What People Are Saying About
Lean Forward into Your Life

"I found *Lean Forward into Your Life* easy to put down. In fact I would put it down at least 20 times an hour. On every page, Mary Anne Radmacher holds up a mirror with angles on each side challenging the reader to examine their thinking and to ask, 'Are my thought processes presently working for me?' The reader is asked to lean forward as if to see his or her own life better, and ponder the risk of introspection. *Lean Forward into Your Life* is a must read, if you are willing to scrutinize how you have life figured out."
  —Von Hansen, National Sales Trainer

"I have worked with Mary Anne for three years and after having read her book can attest that she does indeed 'lean forward into life' in the presence of the inmates she worked with. Mary Anne is a testimony to the concepts she writes about here. I am fortunate to be associated with her generous heart, spirit, and brilliant mind. When I read her book, I laughed, cried, and pondered often. This book has to be taken in bites. It is too substantial to just breeze through."
  —Fay A. Gentle, Transition Coordinator, Oregon State
  Correctional Institution

"Lean Forward. Or Fall Forward. Or Stumble Forward. It doesn't matter. Here's the best part: in this gem of a book, life is not about correct answers. It's all about showing up. Mary Anne's writing is a great invitation to be present. And to embrace and celebrate the extraordinary in the ordinary."
  —Terry Hershey, author of *Sacred Necessities, Soul Gardening,*
  and *Go Away, Come Closer*

"As an artist, my work depends on an inspired and creative state of mind, not always easy to find in this hectic world. While my artistic inspiration comes from nature, I have found in these pages solace for sad times, strength for times of confusion and doubt, and laughter to lighten my days."

—Susan Bourdet, artist and writer

"Some years ago in Southern California I entered a shop and was drawn to a display of unique cards. The words were insightful and poetic, the lettering distinctive and artistic. 'Poetic art,' I thought and bought the card for myself. I still have it. It was the first of many Mary Anne cards I have gifted myself with, as well as those I love. How delightful to discover Mary Anne years later and to become engaged in her uncommon work and wisdom. *Lean Forward into Your Life* is not only poetic art, it is memoir at its most unveiling, wrapped in Mary Anne's gentle guidance for living a fuller, generous life. This is a book of healing and grace meant to give to one's friends and, yes, to give as a gift to oneself. Bravo!"

—Jane Kirkpatrick, author of *A Clearing in the Wild* and *A Land of Sheltered Promise*

Lean forward into your Life

begin each day
as if it were
on purpose

mary anne radmacher

Conari Press

First published in 2007 by Conari Press,
an imprint of Red Wheel/Weiser, LLC

With offices at:
500 Third Street, Suite 230
San Francisco, CA 94107
www.redwheelweiser.com

ISBN-10: 1–57324–298–5
ISBN-13: 978–1–57324–298–1

LIBRARY OF CONGRESS CATALOGING-IN-PUBLICATION DATA
Radmacher, Mary Anne.
  Lean forward into your life : begin each day as if it were on purpose /
Mary Anne Radmacher.
    p. cm.
  ISBN 1-57324-298-5 (alk. paper)
    1. Conduct of life. 2. Intentionalism. 3. Radmacher, Mary Anne. I. Title.
  BF637.C5R328 2007
  158—dc22   2006100564

Cover design by Donna Linden
Text design by Maxine Ressler
Typeset in Adobe Garamond
Artwork and hand lettering by Mary Anne Radmacher

Printed in Canada
FR
10 9 8 7 6 5 4

to gina louise bramucci
because you have the courage to go
the compassion to stay.

———————

contents

foreword

Everyone knows that life is tough—for some more than others. My mom always taught me that the true test of your character is how you react when things are going badly. Beginning at a very young age, I remember sitting on Mom's bed having hour-long discussions about life, death, and religion. Mom said that true religion was being true to your family, trying not to hurt anyone, and helping others as much as you can. I can remember having those discussions at the age of ten. Ten years later while I was serving in the army and stationed in Italy, my mother was murdered in her antique shop back home in Hot Springs, Arkansas. I cannot remember dealing with that grief because I had to be strong for my father.

After that horrible tragedy, I established the attitude that I had had my tragedy of a lifetime and that was it for me. On Memorial Day, May 28, 2001, our seventeen-year-old daughter, Thea Kay Leopoulos, was run off the highway by a reckless driver careening out of control, and our precious daughter was killed. Less than a year later, my older brother died of a rare illness. In 2004, my wife's father died on the night of November 27th, the birthday of our oldest son. The day he was buried, my wife Linda's mother died from brain cancer. She was buried three days later . . . on Thea's birthday, December 6th. (And just to add one more note: The day Thea was killed was Linda's brother's birthday.)

Many say that losing a child is the worst thing that can happen. That is true. It blows a hole in your heart and you are never the same. Many people avoid you. Your life as you knew it is over. People think that after a time you should get over it. Every day is a struggle to get up and hopelessness is a feeling you cannot shake. There is nothing you can do to get out of the nightmare and make things the way they were before.

The interesting thing is that those bedtime chats with my mom on death, life, and religion stuck with me. As parents, Linda and I taught our children to never give up on their moral values and to always believe in themselves. Character means to deal with life's adversity by learning from the adversity and to help others with what we learn. When Thea was killed, there was no choice but to practice what we preached, for our boys were watching—and so was Thea.

Linda and I took Thea's seventeen years of light and established the THEA Foundation (*www.theafoundation.org*). The past five years have been nothing short of amazing. Fifty-five scholarships amounting to over $600,000 have been awarded to graduating high school seniors in Arkansas for their talents in the visual and performing arts. We know they will gain the confidence to lean forward into their lives to pursue their dreams.

The thought of leaning forward into life when times are hard seems totally impossible, even if you want to try. But you know— Mary Anne is right. You can lean forward because you must in order to survive in a healthy way. In this motivating book, Mary Anne gives example after example of how she navigated through a difficult childhood and kept on leaning forward throughout her life to become a bright light in this difficult world. Mary Anne set her own circumstances into motion—ones that helped her live a positive life. She articulates how she made the best of a challenging family life by embracing the simple actions of others who gave her gifts of kindness, friendship, and compassion. Instead of focusing on what she did not have, Mary Anne learned to build a positive attitude about life from the outward gestures of love that were shown to her by others. She learned *meaningful answers* to the meaning of life and shares her recipe with us in this book. Mary Anne also shares her poetry and personal journal entries that she kept along the way as a reminder to herself about where she began her adventure and where she is today.

My congratulations to Mary Anne on presenting an outstanding book of her life's experiences and the lessons she learned, and my gratitude to her for generously allowing me a "Thea moment."

—*Paul Leopoulos*

lean forward into your Life

Lean forward into your life. Indeed. Often I embrace this instruction and put my shoulder to the moment. But certainly not always. There are times when, if I were to lean forward, all I would do is fall over. The roots of the word "despair" can be found in old French—a pairing of "down from" and "to hope": to fall down from hope. When I am not leaning forward into my life that is why. Because I am busy falling down from hope. Sometimes the ship of life is pitching so viciously that the best action I can muster is to just sit down and hang on. The storm subsides. I stand up. I look around. I lean forward a little.

My chiropractor, Dr. Colleen McDonough, was helping me recover from a moment in which I had rapidly leaned backward. I'd stepped backward, while walking my dog, into a recessed planting area in the sidewalk. I snapped something in my back. My doctor was being attentive to the details of my life while working to correct the problem. "Now how's that writing going?" she asked. "That book you're working on—what's it called? *Fall Forward into Life?*"

I laughed so hard. The irony of my chiropractor getting the title of my book so wrong and yet so right, struck me as howlingly funny. When I stopped laughing I told her the correct title. She observed that I more frequently seem to leap forward into my life. A running leap, she modified. With your dog along on a leash. Leap. Lean. It's just one letter difference.

A pilot would tell you that a seemingly insignificant lean of a wing will dramatically alter the direction of the plane. Perhaps if a bird could speak it would share that, with the right wind, a little ruffle of a feather may change the way of its flight.

There are many reasons you lean forward on any given day. They are all perfect metaphors for this book. When you're trying to see something better, you lean toward it. When you are listening to someone and can barely hear, you lean in. When the really exciting part of a basketball game comes, you lean forward in your seat. When you're trying to catch, to see, to listen to the best bits—you lean forward.

Lean forward into your life . . . catch the best bits and the finest wind. Just tip your feathers in flight a wee bit and see how dramatically that small lean can change your life.

begin each day
as if it
were on purpose.

*G*o to the self help section of the library. Or bookstore. There you will find protocols, guides, methods. Ten steps to this. Easy solutions to that. Thirty ways to hop, skip, and jump to a more successful, thinner, efficient, purposeful, happier life.

This is not that.

This book is an invitation. A reflection. A mirror. A set of prompts to help you remember the questions you want to ask yourself. An intimate portrait of some of my processes that have allowed me to separate life as it happens to me and life as I choose it. They are such very different things.

So often people discuss purpose as if it were a far off mountain, difficult to see and even more difficult to climb. Purpose is discussed as if it were the one thing that we are to ultimately achieve in our life.

Jan Johnson, my publisher, has said well that things are not only "done on purpose, but with a purpose." I awaken with my purpose. I bring my purpose to every party. I have the choice of applying my purpose to every set of events and enthusiasms of my life. My purpose. The unique intention that only I bring.

You know that feeling of being completely energized, which occurs when you are doing something you absolutely love? That thing that might make others tired, weary, but you could do for hours, and then get up the next day and do it all over again? *That* thing probably has a lot to teach you about your purpose. When people speak of being "in sync," when things are flowing or a part of a groove. What they could say, instead, is "I am acting in complete accordance to my purpose and it makes everything sing."

Life is the biggest schoolroom there is. Show up. Take notes. Notice the details so you gain mastery over the skills, talents, and abilities that all comprise your special purpose. Writing notes to yourself is one of the finest ways to come to a deeper understanding of your purpose. Here are some suggestions.

Write to make sense of life experiences. Write to learn as much as you can from all the challenges and the joys. Write because words and ideas are fascinating. Write because exploring concepts is play. Write to synthesize explorations and make them practical. Write to become the best version of yourself. Write to inspire, motivate, comfort, facilitate, discover, communicate. In the process of seeking empowerment, empower others. In this scratching, this making marks, encourage others to make their own mark. Write to discover everything you (already deeply) know about your purpose. It's waiting for you.

uncovering
your
purposeful
beginnings

n the classes I teach, Writing Places and Wordshops, I often ask participants to write the story of their mythological creation. Nearly every tribe and civilization that we can name has their own set of creation myths. It explains their unique presence. The terrain. The history of the tribe. Creating your own personal myth is a remarkable journey. It's digging into your purpose. Let me share my own creation myth.

"Entirely too hot!"

"Entirely too high!"

"By all our heads I swear this will turn sunset to a crisp."

"Stop your murmuring and just complete your tasks!" Umbria chastised the rising criticizers.

"You don't think this fire is large enough already?"

"You know size is irrelevant; it's the density of the burn we always look for. Don't be stingy. I know you've not poured yours in yet."

Vitae was embarrassed at being caught. She retreated to the wavy edges of the fire. Appropriately corrected, she humbly reached into her boodle bag and pulled the bottled essence for which she was named. As a single drop entered the fire the core flame leapt higher than Vitae's tall head.

"Only one drop?" Umbria asked.

Shamed, again, this time by her lack of generosity, Vitae poured lavishly—and stepped quickly back from the rising heat. Years later this extra portion of vitality (for which Vitae could take credit) would sustain the breath of this fiery spirit.

Umbria kept her invitations flowing. She calculated on her fingers, "All right, yes! Compassion, Intention, Chaos, Camaraderie, Intimacy, Loyalty, Vision . . . and had Creativity come?" Oh, yes.

Of course. She came in that silly disguise of hers that many mistake for discipline. Now . . . oh, yes!

She called out, "Calculation! Prosperity, Strength and Well-being! Come on. It's nearly time."

While it was somewhat unorthodox, the latecomers all came and piled their offerings in the keeping of Strength—the intensity of the heat had become too much for the rest of them.

"Are we done yet?" Calculation inquired.

"Almost," she impatiently assured. "Would somebody call for Attentiveness and Gentleness? I need them to add something."

Umbria was still deciding what from her bag to bestow—balance or insight. It seemed silly to contribute balance into a fire of this magnitude. The flames were licking the sun and the clouds had begun to complain bitterly. Clearly the only choice they had was to begin a deluge—which tempered the flames slightly. Thereafter this spirit would love all water, especially walking in the rain.

As Gentleness, at some personal peril, added her silken threads, she heard, "Isn't it time yet?" in choired unison.

Umbria gasped at the error of her own long consideration. She knew such an overdue pause would forever compel the belly in which this fire burned to be late. Such things happen. Perhaps insight would help. Umbria tossed her slivers and shards of insight into the flames. In an instant the tower of heat was reduced to a molten coal. Intention and Chaos grabbed the cradle and deftly slipped it under the newly compressed ball of fire. Then they swung the crib back and forth while the others stood in a circle. Following a familiar form they sang their ageless invitation. Soon they heard from the other side of the world.

"It's a girl, Mrs. Radmacher. Does she have a name?"

"Yes, her father and I will name her Mary Anne."

I was oblivious to the inquiry until second grade.

"No! They are my parents, not my grandparents." I was certainly used to them as my parents. The last of my grandparents had died when I was five, and I did not come to understand grief in regard to my grandfather's passing. Only relief. He was described by the non-religious members of my family as some kind of "crazy bastard." Perhaps even the religious family members found it within their experience to levy the same charge against him.

My curiosity pushed beyond its civil limit, I finally asked, "Why? *Why* do you think they are my grandparents?"

The answer was apparent to all but me.

"They are so old."

So old. So old. It was true. Amorous in their anticipation . . . I was the twenty-fifth wedding anniversary celebration to Hawaii that my parents never took. Oddly, I think my mother never really forgave my birth for cheating her of what would have been her first time out of the Pacific Northwest. At least she chose to have me. She was receiving endless unsolicited advice to have me aborted for the sake of her health. She was forty-four. She had a history of miscarriages. Both of my parents insisted that when they married they wanted five children. I would make the fifth, if I survived.

And I did. Against a host of odds. My mother's general health was challenged, and the two packs of cigarettes she smoked each day became a challenge for me. It was mitigated, somewhat, by the two glasses of scotch on the rocks she would imbibe before five. . . .

Oh, what we didn't know then—in 1957—about fetal health and the life-time effects of smoking and drinking while pregnant.

The nine-month lounge act I enjoyed in my mother's belly introduced me to a world bronchially challenged from the word go. At nineteen months old I had a menu of illness offerings: scarlet fever, pneumonia, this and that—the list eludes my accurate memory. Poor care added staph infection to the masterpiece of illness, like a malicious single stroke of red across the painting.

My oldest sister, a nursing student, was home on a break, looked at me for ten seconds, and called the head of pediatrics at Oregon's Health Sciences University. That call saved my life. I was immediately transferred. Months later I was released from a group of loving people whom I had come to view as my family.

That hospital staff had posted twenty-four-hour volunteer duty with me as I was in intensive care alone. Residents reviewed their reports aloud. Students read their textbooks to me. Doctors and nurses read reports *and* children's stories. Doctors would poke their noses into my room and ask me to repeat what had just been announced over the loudspeaker. I did so, verbatim. This was more a developmental exercise for me than a neccessity for them. It certainly was foundational to the way I listened to words.

When I was placed in a normal room, I wondered, at first, who the civilians were who were not dressed in scrub green or white, but who visited me and seemed interested in my progress. I slowly sorted the details of my blood relationship to these guests. This experience would serve as a life-long habit of choosing my own family, rather than simply accepting the bounds of family that blood dictates.

At the going away party, which the staff gave me, I was gifted with a yellow, soft, stuffed elephant. It was made of the same kind of looping of which bedspreads were made. Like overstuffed tatting. I don't know the word for the technique. Bedspreads of this sort are now considered antiques.

The elephant and I were inseparable. Yet in all the time I had it, I had no memory of its source, its beginning place. I had, in fact, no recollection of my time in the hospital at all until much later in my life, until the experience was fully informed by my older sister. The elephant had simply always been with me; it traveled with me, slept with me. I frequently ventured out of doors with that elephant, and it had its own place in my favorite tree. I would jam it under my shirt as I shimmied up the trunk and then place it on its perch where it could view the world along with me. In my memory, its name was the force of its comforting presence, and while I must have called it something, I do not remember giving it a name.

I knew none of the above hospital details until my oldest sister visited me for the fourth time in her life—the first being that visit of which I have just written, the second being my mother's funeral, the third being the visit to officially determine the level of dementia visited upon my father's mind by alzheimer's disease, and the fourth being a few years ago. It was on that fourth visit that I thanked her for all the stories she read to me when I was a wee lass. I had, for decades, attributed my vocabulary and love of books to my oldest sister whom I recalled read to me incessantly when I was a toddler.

"No," she confessed, "it was not me." And then she spun the tale of my illness, my life hanging in a balance for months. The story captivated me, and suddenly made so many nonsensical things about me make sense (things like my precocious vocabulary, my love of new words, my habit of repeating phrases verbatim, and so on). It also disappointed me. How could I have gone through over forty years without anyone telling me such a significant thing about my own life? I asked her.

"I guess no one thought it was important that you should know" she answered. Ah, the odd bits of information families choose to keep from each other.

I don't recall taking my elephant to school, except maybe for show and tell. When I was in fourth grade, my brother left his electric blanket on, crumpled. An electric blanket on an unmade bed in a tinder box of a messy room. A room just across the hall from mine.

The house burned from the roof through to the structure of the second floor. Everything I owned—my art, my writings, all my origami paper brought to me from Japan by my third grade teacher, my clothes—burned. I wept only for one thing. The yellow elephant.

That summer was the only summer my father took me anywhere in the city. He bought a pass to the Portland Zoo. The pass came with a zoo key. The story would be more tidy if the color of the key was yellow. The key was red. Each display had a prerecorded message about the animals, their native habitat, their eating habits. One listened to these messages by inserting the zoo key. The red elephant. My father took me to the zoo a number of times that summer. He should have been sleeping, for he was a graveyard-shift manager at a heavy equipment manufacturing plant. Trying to object to my making a single dart to the elephant exhibit by asserting there were all kinds of things we *could* see—he finally succumbed.

My last visit might still be remembered to this day by the adults that were there. Packy was my favorite elephant, my favorite creature in this structure of fences and yards and pens. I'd participated in a contest to name him. My name, which I cannot recall, was not chosen. But still, Packy was my favorite.

I was aware of murmurs from the crowd around me. Only in retrospect do I know they were saying things such as, "It's like they're speaking to each other," and "Look, that elephant is just staring right at that little girl."

I reached my hands out over the rails, my little body splayed over the double metal railing, my dad holding on to my feet so that I would not go sliding down the cement cliff lining the elephants' area.

Packy raised himself up on this hind feet, his trunk seemed to fly in the air like a restrained bird. And he called to me. A resonant trumpet of a call. And then he thundered himself down and, to the amazement of every one but me, Packy kneeled. His great, soft, leathery, tree-trunk-like legs bent, and that creature bowed to me.

I bowed back as well as I could manage. In much the same way it did not occur to me to think of my parents as old, it did not seem to me that this exchange was in any way odd.

The elephant rose, turned, and disappeared in the interior of the elephant's complex. My dad gently tugged my feet and slid me back over the bars and helped me to the ground. The crowd's tongues were murmuring. My father and I did not speak of it. Not then. Not ever.

"Let's go home, Sissy," he said.

We never went back.

*a*fter being in town a few short weeks, it seemed like Frankie had been in the community for a long time. As if she were exactly where she belonged. And she would tell anybody she was.

A mother who adored her grown children who had children of their own, she was ready for a different kind of life. A lighter life. Without so much "stuff" and only obligations that she would choose, even on a sunny day. This is the life she had created for herself in this small seaside community.

I enjoyed a connection with Frankie. While we were decades apart, we shared some fundamental views, among them, a commitment to the environment. When I started working on energy alternatives as a means to oppose oil leases off the coasts of Oregon and Washington, Frankie jumped right in. She loved that I was working to create solutions, not simply saying no to oil development off our coast. We worked together as volunteers for several years.

Frankie was a remarkable asset in any meeting. She listened attentively, and when she spoke, it was to say the hard thing. She let other people say the easy things. She saved her voice for the truths that everyone knew but didn't have the nerve to say. Frankie was never short on nerve. When I'd thank her she'd brush it off and just say, "Ah, the truth is the truth. Some folks just have a hard time wrapping their lips around it."

Not Frankie.

That is, not until the truth was about her health.

She started missing meetings, making commitments to activities and then not showing up. I called her because this was not her style and I was suspicious. She brushed off the concern saying she was just tired. I pressed her and continued to press until she finally went to the doctor.

In a playful but dreadfully dark way Frankie let me know she'd never be taking my advice again. If I hadn't forced her to see a doctor she'd be blissfully waking to happy days. But since I'd sent her into the arms of medical bad news, *now* she had six months, maybe, to live—and pancreatic cancer to deal with. "No more insistent suggestions from you!"

Awful. Awful news. Well, as testing progressed the news got worse. Frankie was now speaking of weeks, not months. Characteristic of her philosophy of retired life, she wanted to die simply, without a lot of stuff and only obligations to which she was most committed. She gathered a rather small circle of associates. I was among them. She laid down the rules in her fashion—truthfully and without qualification. She had just a few rules:

"One. No assholes allowed. I've put up with them all my life. Now that I'm dying, I don't have to. So if somebody comes and they're an asshole, I'm not spending my dying breath on them. You can tell them anything you want. Just don't bring them to me.

"Two. I get to listen to whatever I want. That means the music I want. Or quiet. And when I want to listen to quiet it means I don't want to talk to you, either. Nothing personal; I just want quiet.

"Three. I get to eat whatever I want. If I want it and we don't have it—you'll do your best to get it. If you can't, I'll understand. But I'd love for you to try. And, also, if I don't want to eat, you won't make me. None of the 'it's good for you' business. I'm telling you right now what's good for me."

People could sign on under Frankie's rules or not. She made it very clear it was *her* party. I was in the rotation several times in those last days. Toward the end I had to lie close to Frankie because she had little breath to put behind her words. Mostly she talked and I listened.

She asked me to promise her something. She said she knew I'd keep writing and sharing my thoughts with the world. She asked me to remind people of something they should know but kept forgetting. And, while I initially disagreed with Frankie's advice, I came to understand the spirit of it: I can either direct the winds of my history to blow and fill my sails toward a certain course—or, I can allow it to just steer me all over the map. I came to realize that Frankie was suggesting that we can negotiate with our history; come to a creative agreement and then move on with our lives, trimming our own sails in a chosen direction.

Frankie believed that we're responsible for our own memories. That responsibility goes in two ways. First, if you had a childhood for which you did not much care . . . MAKE UP a new one. That's why you have an imagination. Just tell yourself a new story—a story that keeps you from living in the past and being bitter. Do what it takes to be happy with your history. And secondly, be responsible today for the history you are creating. Ask yourself how it is you want to remember this specific thing and then do your best to bring about those memories. In a great difficulty or a perplexing moment, it's a tool of perspective to pause and ask yourself, "How do I want to remember this?" It sings of personal responsibility and the kind of accountability that makes a big person.

I told Frankie I would do it. That I would remind people as often as I had the opportunity. And I have with City Year in Little Rock, Arkansas, a volunteer domestic service program started by President Clinton, as well as with computer marketing professionals in Portland, Oregon, and folks in every spot I've visited and given a speech. Now, I'm telling you the story. I promised and I've kept my promise. And in tough spots I clarify for myself by asking, "How is it I would most like to remember this?"

On the day of Frankie's memorial service, much of that small community shut down. I had my memorial service right next to Frankie and her failing breath. The day of her service I stayed home and memorialized her in my own way. Yes, I cried. And yes, I asked myself how I would like to remember the day of her memorial. I wanted to define the lessons I'd learned by living by Frankie as she died. That day I wrote the text, which has grown into the version that I use today. I wrote:

> live with intention.
> walk to the edge.
> listen hard.
> laugh.
> play with abandon.
> practice wellness.
> continue to learn.
> appreciate your friends.
> choose with no regret.
> do what you love.
> live as if this is all there is.

She did. And I aspire to.

Over the years this text has appeared through my company in posters in people's offices, homes, school rooms, and lockers. It's on web sites, been featured in newspapers and city mission statements, read at memorial services, and used in graduation speeches. Here is the most recent incarnation of the text:

> live with intention.
> walk to the edge.
> listen hard. play with abandon.
> practice wellness. laugh. risk love.
> continue to learn. appreciate your friends.
> choose with no regret.
> fail with enthusiasm.
> stand by your family.
> celebrate the holidays that make sense.
> lead or follow a leader. do what you love.
> live as if this is all there is.

Richard Kesler, a "Macgyver" kind of man to whom I gave my father's pocketknife—because he knew so many helpful things to do with it and because he is a father figure to so many kids—has a different view toward his history. He never re-writes his history. He turns his experiences into types of tales, or parables, so that he and others might continue to learn from them. He explains his telling of his own history in this way: "It's not a scar, it's a story."

> Anyone who has been blessed with having children in their
> lives will know this story well. My three daughters have

enriched my life with six grandkids. The oldest is Austin. He is the real author of the quote above. I have a few reminders left from a well-spent youth permanantly etched onto my face, leg, and back. They are scars from car accidents, sports injuries, and the every-man scars we all get just living. My grandkids, like all kids, don't see me as just a person. One day I'm a horse giving rides to a place only a child's eyes can see. On another day I'm an amusement park ride, flying them through the air. And, of course, I am always Superman. On one particular day, lying on the floor, I am a racetrack. My grandson drives his toy cars up and down the three surgical pieces of artwork that resemble railroad tracks covering the length of my back. He asks how they got there. I answer in short versions. Just enough to satisfy his curiosity about each spot. Then, stopping to touch my face, then looking at my leg, then retouching the scars on my back, he finally assesses, "You know, Grandpa, you sure have a lot of stories."

From then on, inspired by Austin, I would tell anyone who asked about a particular remnant from my youth, "It's not a scar, it's a story."

Intention is not groggy in the morning. The day is met with a particular enthusiasm. The possibilities of the day are partners—not adversaries. Intentional living recognizes that, while accidents happen, life is not an accident. Days are built choice by choice. Intention savors moments of peaceful contemplation equally with production initiative. Intention knows each moment of the day as a precious investment.

Life is not a series of accidents, and you are not a victim. You can exert power and influence over your own actions, attitudes, and resources.

Be honest.
Speak directly.

Recognize it is more appropriate (at times) to remain quiet.

Define your person in the context of that which is positive and possible. Do not identify yourself by your shortcomings or that which you are (as yet) unable to do.

Choose your qualities.

You can become the person you long to be. In a very real sense, in your longing—you are already that person. In practical terms, you are a project. A project undertaken by a qualified director . . . you. If you have habits you do not enjoy (study and) find a way to get rid of them. Are there qualifications you need? (learn more about them and) acquire them.

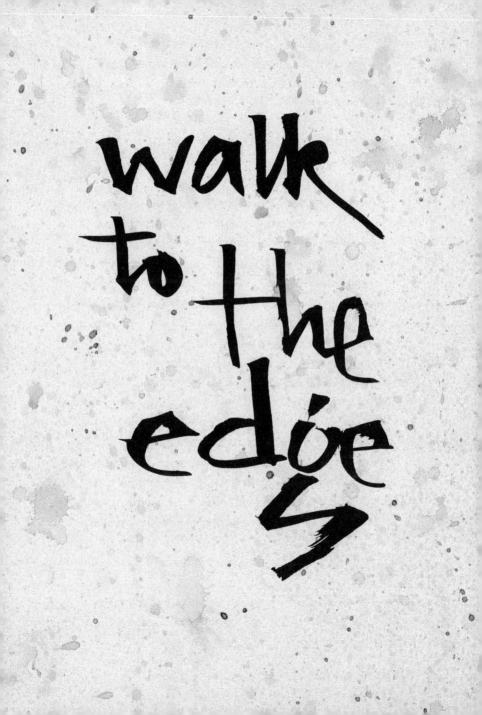

it is not the easy or convenient life for
which i search, but life lived to the edge
of all that i may be.

one often meets their destiny on the way to somewhere else. at first
glance it may appear too hard. look again. always look again.

i awakened. isn't that a wonderful statement? i awakened. oh that
it were true in every cell of my being. i awakened! i no longer slept.
i did not draw down the shades of my spirit and remain forever
slumbered to the vitality of life. i set aside numbness and even
willingly choose pain over not feeling. ah. there's a lesson here. is
it the self-punisher who would contrast a willingness for pain over
numbness? i see the reach but i must invent a new internal dynamic.
i would choose joy. i would choose JOY over pain.

asked a participant in my wordshop, Art for the Creatively
Reluctant, if he was happy with his work. He responded,
"How would I know if I am happy with it if I have never
done it before? I have nothing to compare it to."

Implicitly this asserts it is only by comparison or contrast that
we make assessment and assertion. (I am tempted to measure
experience against experience and myself against other people.)

Where do I fall on the continuum? If that person is excellent
then must I be less than excellent? And if this experience is peak,
does that mean the elevation of this other experience is lower?
Can we not stand atop many tall mountains and savor each of
their views without comparison? Could my guest have taken a
snapshot of his immediate feelings and simply allowed himself to

be "happy" with words, with creating, with the enthusiastic support around him? Apparently, not so easily. He required a frame of reference, a means of comparison in order to feel good about his creating.

Comparison and qualifiers. "You are this, but you are not that." Or "This experience contained this, but it was absent that." This is how we encounter disappointment. Comparison breeds expectation, and expectation envisions. If the actual sight is different from the vision, then rather than producing surprise or delight, it creates disappointment. So in this day and then day by day collected into the larger frame which is the picture, the snapshot of my life, may I awaken with anticipation, not expectation, that I may experience delight rather than disappointment.

Walk to the edge.

Said another way (as it has been said many other ways): live boldly. Not an endorsement of recklessness or cavalier behavior, but an urging to push personal limits. Live boldly, not loudly. Not at the highest volume on the dial, but dialed to the best reception. What a grating experience to listen long to a radio station that is not dialed to the best reception. One must strain to hear even incorrectly—the programming comes in and goes out. You are uncertain if the missed details were key to understanding. What *did* you miss? Being dialed in—fully receiving the signal—that's what it is to live boldly. And that is what it takes to walk to the edge.

I visited the cliffs of a moor in Ireland. The fencing (designating the safe viewing place from the step just before "over the edge") was very un-fence like. Really more like the small fence used around a flower bed. More decorative than functional. I remember being startled by the innocuous nature of the fence. As if it were a gentle suggestion that you might not want to travel beyond this point but if you are interested in going to the edge and hanging over, we wouldn't want to prevent you the experience. Yes. Those very thoughtful Irish. I did walk to the edge. And I did peer over. Not for long, for the drop took my breath. Not steep; straight down. But what a view.

Walk to the edge. Push your boundaries. Question your assumptions—those that are your own and those that others presume for you to undertake. Take all your expectations, which are kept in little boxes, and stack the boxes in the form of a ziggurat, or pyramid. And then step up and to the edge of it. Einstein believed that it is madness to continue the same actions and expect different results.

Walking to the edge is performing an action with the expectation of creating different results. Therefore the action must be different. It is not an invitation to continually make yourself uncomfortable—but rather, to question your comfort ability. What opportunities are missed by simply claiming the action that is most familiar, the one that is easiest to reach from where you're standing?

Conventional wisdom might retort with, "If it ain't broke, don't fix it."

A thing can break slowly. So slowly I don't even notice the break. I simply learn to compensate. Over time I've operated in tried ways with a system which is profoundly dysfunctional and I've not noticed. This happens all the time when people injure themselves. Fractures gradually worsen but the ability to compensate and mask over pain is staggering.

What happens when I walk to the edge? At the cliffs of the moor I lost a good amount of my breath. I was afraid. I moved away from my traveling companion warily, lest his sudden movement, wholly impersonal and not owing to me anything, should accidentally tip me toward a view I would not much care for (accidentally becoming quite personal). I compared the Irish fence structure and my concept of "fence" (developed in a lifetime of living in America) with what a fence is supposed to accomplish. In the moments before my desire of not wanting to fall tiptoed me back over the small fence, I felt a holy and unfamiliar wind. The colors of this majestic wonder compelled my imagination. Not in any other place in Ireland did I have the full impact of islandness than I had standing in this spot, this very vulnerable spot.

So. It may be frightening. Standing at the edge validates or clarifies our values and provides a sense of what is truly important. Loyalty and a sense of trust in our companions is called into question at the edge: one is more inclined to fend for one's own safety than depend, magnanimously, on the good intentions of another. Walking to the edge is something more likely to be done alone than with another or in a group. Walking to the edge becomes a very selective process. Who is at your shoulder or taking on the wind alongside you is very significant. To stand next to that person at the edge requires a great bit of trust. Generally, it's not advisable to walk to the edge as a social setting. The edge is an inappropriate context for gaining group consensus. Consideration by committee takes too long when one is faced with the choice between a few inches to a two hundred foot drop or flat ground behind a small fence.

And what of that drop? What are the consequences of such a fall? Is it correct to assume the results are death? Walks to the edge point out a knowledge base that needs to be filled out. Questions that need to be answered. Assumptions that can be challenged.

The view. After all the other considerations perhaps it is the view, which is the best justification for such steps. "The best place to stand is where everybody else—isn't." Just as the best thing about leading a parade is that there are no hats, trombones, or batons to look around or over. Leading the parade provides the best view. (Leading a parade also provides the best view of you— it's a visible and vulnerable place.)

I am looking at a view—and I give my breath over to it. With grace, it gives my breath back. I determine to do a thing at the edge not *because* it makes me uncomfortable but *in spite* of the fact that it does. I allow that discomfort to instruct me; it is the discomfort of an experience at the edge that is the personal litmus of when it is time to step back behind the fence—or, perhaps, off the edge.

Stretch your usual patterns. (Recognize that habit provides a certain discipline or safety.) Do not become locked behind habit.

Read a type of literature that is unfamiliar to you.

Avoid television for an extended period.

Send an unexpected letter.

See a movie by yourself.

Go a different way.

Try new tastes, colors, smells, sounds, ideas.

Stop affirming, "Oh, I'm not very good at (fill in your particular thing) and then undertake a project as if you are good at that thing.

Introduce yourself to someone you have been wanting to meet.

Recognize the power of your words. Accept that they have a consequence (words build cultures, and preserve and destroy them). Every word has a story and a degree of impact. Do not say of your words, "Oh, they don't matter." They matter a good bit.

there is no silence long enough to keep me from listening to your
heart and celebrating the vastness of your spirit.

remember the difference between looking and seeing
(remember the difference between hearing and listening.)

O ne of my best pals is eight. She advises me on fashion, shares
her opinions on my food choices (many of which she
approves, by the way), and tries to teach me jazz moves that make
me apprehensive about the way she wants me to position my older
self. A pretzel comes to mind. She shares her opinion about the
way I "screw up" my face.

"Why are you screwing up your face like that?" she used to ask
with frequency.

"I'm listening to you."

"But why does it look like it hurts?" was her well-founded
question.

"Because I'm listening to you so hard."

"Maybe you should listen a little lighter—you're going to give
yourself wrinkles."

Her advice continues to be reasonably sound. A recent check in
the mirror bears out her assessment. Between laughing hard and
listening hard, I've tracked some well-earned line miles across my
face.

When I listen to someone I hear their words in the same way
I hear my own words when I am typing quickly. I have a tactile
encounter with each word in order to type it accurately. If I were
to rewrite this phrase I might consider amending it to, "listen hard
and well," for there's a little magic in listening well—to hearing

what is being said as well as what is not being said. Oh, volumes have been written on why it is that we come to have so many misunderstandings. But not in this volume. I still have many misunderstandings with my words—bring offense when none is meant. I have much to learn on this note.

Life experiences and maturity help us to know when listening hard and well means discounting some of what is being heard. It means coming to understand that one thing said can actually *mean* something else. This is how humor works. And gentle suggestions.

For weeks in advance of my fifth birthday I was very busy communicating with everyone in my family that I would like a birthday party with my neighborhood friends, a birthday cake with candles and balloons. I didn't even mention presents. I thought the party would be enough. I had just completed a string of birthday parties for my pals and I thought that it would be the finest thing to turn five with a party of my own.

My suggestions were met with disinterest and deferral. I waged a campaign. I sought justifications. I offered strategies to make the party easier. I would concede the balloons. No. Not yet. Everyone thought maybe a party would be a good idea when I turned six.

I was clear. I would give up birthday parties for many subsequent years but, just like my friends, I wanted a party when I turned five. I was unsuccessful in all my lobbying. And I was one disappointed four-year-old.

There was one bright spot on the day of my birthday. My sister said that I could go to the library and check out three books. Three! At one time. Now that I was five I guess this was the privilege that came with maturity. It wasn't fully able to assuage my loss of the long-hoped-for party, but it came darn close.

I had selected two books when suddenly my sister became urgent about wanting to go.

"I've only got two books."

"You can only read one at a time," she observed. This was not precisely accurate but I could see she was inexplicably in no mood to negotiate. I wasn't leaving without three books so I threw my last deliberation to chance and grabbed a book off the shelf.

I'd seen folks launching kites and it occurred to me from the way my sister was hauling me home that maybe if I'd had a tail she might have been able to let me out on a string and flown me like a kite. This girl was in one kind of hurry.

It seemed odd to me that she insisted on taking my books as we came to the steps of our house. More negotiating. They were mine. *All three.* I handed them over. Distracted, I pushed through the door to a torrent of leaping children, streamers and balloons, and staccato screams of "Surprise! Surprise, surprise!"

I was surprised all right. There was a banner over the mirror above the mantle announcing "It's your birthday!!!" I didn't think I was the one who needed reminding; it was my family who had all appearances of forgetting that I was turning five.

I surveyed the room, speechless. Yes. There were balloons. A cake with unlit candles on the table. Wow! A pile of presents. What mad plan had this been? I was stunned. My entire family had lied to me for weeks. Liars, all of them? If you can't believe your family, who can you believe? I wondered. The neighbor children had stopped leaping. The calls of surprise had dwindled to bewilderment. Everyone in the room stared at me as my face crumpled and I began to cry. Steve West, my best pal, came to offer me the only solace he had: "Whataya crying for? It's your birthday."

Again what? Was I the one who needed to be reminded? I had asked. For weeks. I had communicated clearly what I wanted. What joke was this? I ran into the room adjacent to the living room and helped myself into the linen closet where I shut the door behind me and cried.

Graciously, someone laid the arm down on an album and started in with games. Without me. A few minutes later my sister came in with tissues. She offered that nobody meant to hurt my feelings—they wanted to surprise me. I explained that the only surprise that I had was that I was surprised everyone had forgotten my birthday and then I was surprised that everyone had lied. Neither one of us can now remember how long it took her to talk me out of the linen closet. But she eventually did. Just in time for cake.

Life experiences draw certain subtleties for us. They expand our ways of listening and give us other tools for understanding what people are saying and what they are not saying; what it is they say they want and what it is they really want.

It was clear what I wanted. My family wanted something different. I learned, as I grew older, that this is not just the way of families, but of all relationships. Even when you "listen hard" you can be unclear as to what someone really wants.

Wouldn't you just imagine that it was quite some time before I could actually enjoy the process of a surprise party. Actually, I've never really enjoyed a surprise party. Perhaps some day I'll learn a new way.

There are many people whose words have influenced me. Some of those words, and some of their stories, are salted throughout this book. As I contemplated the effects of those words upon me, I turned the thinking upside down and wondered if I could discover a stranger upon whom my words had some sort of effect. I am grateful for my loyal customers who graciously take the time to let me know the place my words have in their life. But I wanted to go in search of someone who lived with intention, used my words, but didn't know me. I went to the Internet and entered some of the key words from the "Live with Intention" text. Numbers of websites responded to the search. One particular site caught my attention. There my search began and ended.

"The Best of What's Left" was a blog written by a fifty-something professional man who had recently lost his lifelong wife, partner, and friend to a battle with cancer. Rather than long succumbing to the sorrow of his loss, he started questioning his values, considering his aspirations and decided, yes, to make "the best of what's left." He purposed to leave his chosen field and accept a position, which would travel him all over the globe. Ultimately he even set aside those structures in order to construct a life based upon his rediscovered dreams.

This man, who had featured the text of my writing on his site, did indeed seem to live out the tenets of that writing with enthusiasm. He announced to the world that he supposed the woman who wrote "Live with Intention" was probably 106 and her idea of walking to the edge might be passing on her Metamucil for a day. I told him I would not let him forget that assessment. Ever. And now, it's there in black and white. Again. I did immediately inform him that while I thought there was nothing wrong with being 106 (I hope I get to find out!) and that I'd never actually *had* Metamucil, I could lay claim to having written the words he'd featured on his blog. This began a delightful and challenging communication with a person who has the courage to question the assumptions of his life, ask himself the real heart of his dreams, and act on them. It turns out Michael R. Wigal inspires a lot of people to live with intention, including me. He shares this story from his life experience called, "Leaning Forward into Your Foxhole."

In a previous life I was a young second lieutenant in the 82nd Airborne Division. (I'm a pacifist now, but life is about transition.) Field Artillery to be exact, a Forward Observer. My battalion commander was a hard-driving, up-from-the-ranks guy by the name of Bobby J. Godwin. We called him the "Godfather." He was a man who drove his troops through a combination of fear and respect. I was afraid of him. (And people said I was one of his favorites!) But, he would always urge us to do better. One of his constant sayings was, "I want you leaning forward in the foxhole." Those words stuck with me through the years. I have taken a "leaning forward in the foxhole" approach to life.

This is not a combat story. I never saw combat (thankfully!). It was a training thing at Ft. Bragg, North Carolina. The year must have been 1974. There was a battalion-wide contest to determine who was the best Forward Observer (F.O.). That would be one of three guys, as there were three Firing Batteries (six guns each) in the battalion. (While this information is not necessarily germane to the story, it's interesting background, especially for guys.)

Even though the F.O. operates pretty much by himself in terms of identifying targets, determining the target's location as accurately as possible, and calling that location (via radio) back to the guns, in those days it took a fairly complex system to actually fire a round that had any chance of getting near the target. Once the F.O. had what he thought was a fairly good read on the target's location (using map and compass back then), he called the estimated coordinates to the Fire Direction Center. There, in a tent, maybe six other guys worked to plot those coordinates on a kind of map. The map showed the surveyed location of the guns and the perceived location of the target. Through a series of calculations the direction and distance of the target from the guns was calculated. The settings for the guns were then called to the Executive Officer (X.O.), who was directly responsible for relaying the settings and insuring they were set correctly on the guns. The gunners and assistant gunners and others in the team did that. They also prepared the rounds for firing and loaded the piece. Once satisfied, the X.O. would fire one round from one gun (the base piece). Everyone would wait to see where the round landed. If it was a little off, the F.O. "adjusted fire" until a round hit within a certain area of the target (usually a junked tank or truck or something). Important note, the howitzer is an "area weapon." You don't have to actually hit the thing directly. You just have to get near it. Within ten yards was considered successful. A Fire Mission would be pretty quick if you could make the adjustments and "hit" the target within two moves from the original call.

You can see how hard it was to do all this quickly. Of course, quickly was what it was all about. And accurately. A lot depended upon the responses of others. Like so much else in life, the results were not entirely in our individual control.

If a guy was having trouble at home or financial problems or woman problems or a million other things, he might not be fully involved. It was the job of the Godfather, the Battalion Commander, to pass down to the officers and men below the importance of doing this thing well. So the Godfather was all geared up as were we lowly Second Lieutenants. It was a chance for us to shine as well as a chance for him to get bragging rights as to the efficiency of his battalion. All very Gung Ho.

Naturally, I felt I was the best F.O., probably in the world, so I was keyed up. As we awaited the call on the radio to start, the Godfather's voice came over: "I want everyone leaning forward in their foxholes on this." I didn't win that day. I got second on what to this day I consider a bad call. However, in the long run, I won.

Here is my take on what he meant and how it applies to life. The Godfather wanted our undivided attention. Every eye focused forward. Every action geared toward success. No wasted motions, no distractions.

A foxhole is two things: a protective position and a fighting position. You sleep in it, you work in it, you eat in it, you live in it. But, that isn't why you are in it. The reason you are in a foxhole is "out there." It is the job of the soldier to deal with the thing "out there." While we could, let's not talk about the brutishness of war, the inhumanity. That's a given. Just to the lesson.

What Bobby Godwin meant that day was:
live with intention.
walk to the edge.
listen hard.

I got that. I got that then and I get that now. For us to have a meaningful, satisfying, purposeful life we have to deal with the thing "out there."

Of course life is far more complicated than this example. I only had to fear the wrath of the Godfather. That was enough. Made things very clear. It was relatively easy.

I didn't go to school, get married, have a son, work or play in a (literal) hole in the ground. But, we do have a tendency to build foxholes around us in everyday life. We want safety, assurance, insurance, protection for our families, job safety, IRAs, side-crash airbags, "born-on dates" on our beer cans. It builds a bunker mentality. But, it is an illusion. Security is an illusion. It only takes one thing (and for all your efforts to be safe you never see that particular thing coming), and it's over.

So we have to deal with the "out there." Take life on. Engage. That is why we are here in the first place.

Practice listening. Choose a place, a conversation, an audiotape, a meeting—and pay attention to the point at which you stop listening to the other and start listening to your own thoughts.

Discipline yourself to summarize either to yourself or to the person to whom you have been listening. Step outside at the start of your day and listen. Pause long enough to listen at the end of the day. How are the sounds different? What do they tell you about where you live?

Practice.

live boldly. laugh loudly. love truly.
play as often as you can.
work as smart as you are able.
share your heart as deeply as you can reach.
    as you awaken
    may your dreams
    greet you by name and
    may you answer, "yes."
as you walk
may all your angels
gather at your shoulders and
may you confidently know
they stand with you.
    as you rest
    may all your endeavors
    know contentment and peace.

My two finest teachers in regard to play have been a stout labrador, who is four, and a fiery red head who is now eight. These two have conspired to invite, "let's play together" to spring strongly and easily to my lips. I've come to understand that really means the same thing as, "I love you." Those three words come forward—open doors to a stronghold, a winter-wilderness fortress. They come forward saying, "I offer you my own best strength, in spending playful time with you, in loving you I offer you the same comforts, security, abilities, and opportunities which I offer myself. My doors are swung wide for you and here is the key. Come to my castle never as a prisoner or emissary but as a

reigning monarch of your own wild kingdom. And only and ever
the title you hold within my walls is
                    "treasured friend."

What I appreciate about my red-headed friend, Taylina, and my
dog, Judah, is their loyalty partnered with their truth telling. Both
of them let me know in their own gentle ways, when I am being
less than myself, when I am not feeling well . . . and they stay by
me, nonetheless. They don't really need me, but they want me.
That's the finest quality of presence. A function of choice, not of
obligation or requirement. Funny, reflective, compassionate, attentive. Never stingy with their affection. Smart enough to get me to
do what they want me to do and make it seem like my idea.

There are many things that Judah teaches me that Taylina
can't—because his ears are longer, like velvet, and he has four legs
instead of two. These are simply anatomical advantages. However, Taylina can wield a paintbrush in a way Judah can only envy.
Her creativity and ingenuity inspire me all the time. And Taylina
dances in ways that leave both Judah and me breathless.

They both teach me how and invite me to play. Taylina invites
me into active, creative, moving play. And Judah takes me to the
open grass and helps me play in stillness. He forces me, by virtue
of his one-hundred-and-thirty-five-pound-labrador frame sitting
down and not wishing to move, to smell the wind and the scents
it carries, to notice the smaller creatures at play, and to simply be
patient and enjoy the weather—whatever that weather might be.

My friend Von informs me that grass is the outdoor scent
museum for dogs. In much the same way I would not want to be
tugged away from my wonder at Van Gogh's *Starry Night,* neither

does Judah wish to be hurried in his judicious appreciation for all smells grass. Judah is an able and schooled epicure of grassness. He is also a highly qualified instructor of play.

Jane Kirkpatrick, the award-winning author, is a friend of mine. She's one of the most disciplined writers I know. I can hear her snorting when I say this, but it's true. In the midst of a field of incredible life challenges, Jane diligently ploughs her craft and presents amazing novels set in a historical context. We've mused, on occasion, about the demands of a writing life. In this piece, which Jane wrote just for this book, she muses on the women in her life and what they each taught her about play.

My German grandmother played with abandon. She worked hard, too, raising two families, helping her husband run two photographic studios, and becoming a fine photographer herself. She may have found joy in taking pictures of people and gardens but I never saw her photographs; just my grandfather's. But I know she played because I heard her.

She couldn't read a note of music but she'd been given that rare gift of perfect pitch and the ability to sit before ivory keys and choose chords we all sang to, every Christmas in her four-story Minneapolis home. It's one of my fondest memories, watching her play that high-back piano, the workman's-size muscles of her forearms only slightly out of place on her less than five-foot-tall frame. She also took us to the Hennepin Avenue Methodist Church on Christmas morning where we heard a pipe organ so grand our feet rattled to its throb. Her face, lifted to the heavens as she sang Charles Wesley hymns, was filled with joy. Music made her play.

My older sister played too. She loved snowmobiling especially in spring powder up on McArthur Rim, the edge of an old volcano in Oregon's Cascade Mountains. She turned work into play by feeding hay to their many horses with her four-wheel vehicle pulling a wagon behind her, sometimes with a grandchild riding high atop the alfalfa bales, a dog or two trotting along beside. Her greatest play was on horseback. She could have the worst day ever then transform it all by spending an hour in the saddle riding through rabbit brush and beneath Ponderosa Pine looking out over the seven snowcapped mountains of the Cascades outside their Central Oregon ranch.

When at forty-eight she was diagnosed with a rare multi-system disorder that rendered her muscles so out of her control that in her final days we often had to lift her eyelids just so she could see us, it was being set up on her horse, her feeding tube adjusted while her son held her steady as he sat behind her, that helped her play. She could feel herself alive on top that animal, feel the gelding's muscles move as she leaned toward his neck. She was "centered" she said, her face a wide smile. I worried out loud once to the doctor about her falling off as she leaned so precariously at times, and she said, "It's the greatest joy of her life. Wouldn't you like to be doing what you love right up until your death?" The week before my sister died, she rode her horse sitting in front of her son when in earlier years he would have sat safely in front of her. Roles reversed but the play still there.

My mom played less than anyone that I can remember. As both a nurse and dairy farmer's wife raising three children, she found little time for play. She made lists of tasks. She performed private-duty nursing in my early years, often dressing in that white cap and leaving our farm in the night to help someone else. Later she administered nursing-home services, supervising nurses. She'd come home to the farm, change her clothes then help my dad with "chores."

I do remember my parents getting dressed up for square dancing, something to warm them on cold Wisconsin nights, a blend of music and movement. She liked to crochet and knit and did that while the rest of us listened to stories on the radio. She wouldn't have called that "play"; just making good use of her time.

In later years, her stoic disposition tempered with funny facial expressions gave pleasure to her caregivers in the assisted-living facility where she and my father passed their final days. It was then I discovered that she loved reading and she saw that as play.

As I look back it was inside the comfort of her faith where my mother played the most. She laughed well after church services chatting with her friends. She listened and discussed a pastor's thoughts finding joy in the challenges of new ways of thinking about scripture. She read books, novels even. She attended women's retreats and giggled like a school girl in the comfort of women of faith.

After she died, I found her school autograph book where she listed things she loved as a child. "Violets. Music. Skating." Flowers? Music? Movement? Who knew? We had played music for her in her last hours and her last movement was when she turned her head to the old hymn, "Softly and Tenderly, Jesus is

Calling." She leaned into the music and smiled just before she died.

At my mother's funeral, we found occasion to play despite the confusion over the gravedigger not having time to dig the grave. My nephew, who knew him, called to say he'd seen his back hoe just sitting by the house so why didn't he have time to "dig my grandma's grave." Apologies and plans followed as can happen in a little country cemetery. The grave was dug. But her casket had to be placed in the ground by five strong men rather than the hydraulic system useful with a level grave. Mom and Dad's grave site graced a hillside looking out over a beautiful meadow. "Hang on to my belt here," the undertaker told my brother-in-law. "Keep me from slipping in while I help lower this casket." We watched as that belt got pulled higher and higher and my brother-in-law dug his heels in to the soft dirt to keep the man from tumbling into the tomb. A wedgie of gargantuan proportions occurred right before our eyes.

We finally could not hold back the laughter knowing Mom would be laughing, too, as they settled her casket in the ground without men falling in behind it. Somehow the tears were more cleansing mixed in with laughter.

Music, movement, faith, that's how the women in my life played. They're all gone now and I look back to see the threads of their playing inside the stories of my life.

I love music. My sister and I sang duets when we were young. An aunt gave me piano lessons, but the flute became my instrument of choice in high school. In college I joined a chorus, just one voice in many where I found an easy peace while the world around me swirled with news of war and waning wisdom. Before we moved to our remote ranch where we live now, we bought an old piano, refinished it. We carried it first into our country home. I don't play it much. I like what it reminds me of when I look at it. Instead, I sometimes turn the car volume up as high as it will go, wind the windows down, open the skylight, and let Josh Groban or the Los Angeles Philharmonic or Willie Nelson or Maroon 5 blare away to me and the mule deer as I head home on our twisting reptile road, singing along if the words aren't in Italian.

Movement. My walks apply. I sometimes deprive myself of how good a walk can make me feel, think I have no time, contracts must be met, duty calls. But then the puppy puts his paws on my computer keyboard or sticks his furry face into mine and as my sister with her horses, I find myself alive walking, working the dog, watching him run along the rimrocks while I stride between those ancient reddish rocks and the music of the river. I feel at play then, as much as someone who took up golf or dancing or gardening. I am leaning into life with movement.

My faith. These women leave a legacy of a joyous faith, not one of doom and gloom or waiting for the worst. When I look at this month alone I find I've found the greatest joy in the company of women who would describe themselves as being on a spiritual journey. At a woman's retreat we laughed over lingerie and indigestion and someone noted that surely God must wonder at the things that make us women laugh. At a book signing, I played with women who had not only read my books but so many others that I loved, too. Like a menu of tasty morsels, they listed treasured titles, the characters and themes. Their eyes sparkled as they talked about how stories nurture us, heal us, and make us whole. The titles and images danced around the room as we recalled modern parables. Some days, I call my grandchildren just to hear them tell me of their lives, or I call my women friends and we find laughter over what the dog has done, what our children said, a foolish thing we did. Even reading greeting cards will make me laugh and connect me to a perfect stranger standing beside me at the card shelf. Such playing provides fuel for when I face a loss and I can hear the gasp of grieving of my friends knowing they are there for me though they live miles away.

These moments of connected joy cradled in the faith of understanding describe for me what the Apostle Peter meant when he wrote that we have each "tasted of the Lord's kindness." It is a human thing to play, to taste such kindnesses.

Music, movement, faith: they all speak of intentions offered and received. They say "play with abandon." Doing so lets me lean in not only to the goodness of the world but to my inner world, my memories of strong women and how their playing feeds my soul. Play—with abandon. It's a gift I hope I can pass on.

Every once in a while make no plans. Have the nerve to walk out the door and let possibilities introduce themselves. Wander. Imagine. Stare. Be surprised: parades will find you. Travel—in your armchair, with a book, on a boat, in a car, in your thoughts, on a bike or any vehicle that will take you from the walls of your own knowing to someplace other. Other gestures, smells, words, tastes, views. Look upon the world through windows other than your own. Learn to be good company for yourself. A bit of joy passes by because "there was no one to go with." A party of one is sometimes the best time. Dance by yourself, anywhere there is room in your house. There is something invigorating, even a bit magic, to music, to movement and a touch of laughter. Go ahead: dance. Enjoy participating in the unexpected. A little turn of whimsy is a gift: a quick, cool rain shower on a hot, dusty day. Enjoy flowers for no reason, visit an old friend, greet a stranger, tell a sweet little joke in line at the grocery store. (What did the snail say as he climbed on the back of the turtle? WHEEEEEEEE!!!!) Play can happen anywhere . . . you are the toy. Laugh.

practice wellness

peak quietly to yourself and promise there will be better days. Whisper gently to yourself and provide assurance that you really are extending your best effort. Console your bruised and tender spirit with reminders of many other successes. Offer comfort in practical and tangible ways—as if you were encouraging your dearest friend. Recognize that on certain days the greatest grace is that the day is over and you get to close your eyes. Tomorrow comes more brightly . . .

how do i demonstrate reverence for my being in an ordinary
    day?
honor the possibility awaiting in each day;
celebrate my native enthusiasm;
contribute to the wellness of my being by all my choices;
seize upon the opportunity to serve and contribute to the
    dreams of others;
remove obstacles to the divine expressing itself to me and
    through me by embracing my own spiritual practice;
sing, dance, laugh, walk and rock the world;
pursue excellence in all my choices;
create relentlessly.

get lost: that's how you find your way back to yourself.

perpetrate vast goodnesses on the planet.
    go ahead and cry. let your tears teach you. tears can be stepping
stones to your renewal.

These summary notes from Abraham Maslow's philosophy have been instrumental for me.

step away from the tribe.

be independent: DO NOT work for the good opinion
of others;

do not be attached to specific outcomes;

you can only know your finest self when you intentionally
step aside

from the expectations of the tribe;

let go of governing the actions and attitudes of others.

Unfetter yourself. How is it you choose to become fettered to things? What are fetters precisely? They are part of the equipment attached to load-bearing animals.

The other week I said I was an eagle behaving like a pack mule.

Have the courage to forgive yourself. Have the compassion to forgive others. Forgiveness is a healer. Holding on to resentment, hurt, and blame knits wounds into your bones.

Be specifically grateful. Practice forgiveness as a way to wellness. Be quick to make amends for what you have (or have not) done. Do not apologize as a quick fix or a way to avoid confrontation. Write letters that you will never send. Write your vivid anger slashingly on a page and then burn it and watch the smoke float away. When someone has died, or left in some way, write all the things that were left unspoken. When you need support or tenderness, write to give yourself the words you need. Reach deeply and pick the rose you planted in yourself so long ago.

in each moment seize the opportunity to experience grand wonder
. . . after the wonder, joy comes in.

there is a song so deep within the soul it is only heard as laughter.
from the fountain of our beliefs come the graces of our lives.

hope flies on its own wings,
carried on winds of laughter,
it will always find its way to the
heart it calls home.

laugh. it is the quickest bridge between strangers and the finest path
between friends.

'll tell anybody for certain that owning your own business is
not for the faint of heart. Something outrageously difficult had
just occurred. It was jaw-dropping bad news just when we were
certain that we had heard all the bad news there was to hear. Tony
and I stared at each other. Silent. Breathless. The wretchedness of
the confluence of seemingly tragic business events snapped both
of us and we cascaded into fits of uncontrolled laughter. Gasping
for breath, Tony summarized the situation perfectly:
   *The thing about falling into an old well is that you might
discover*
   You have water after all.

Laugh right out loud. Even if you're the only one laughing.
Write a truly funny moment down, remember it. Spread the joy.
The next time a conversation takes an undesirable turn, share
this thing, which made you laugh. At the very least—you'll
laugh again.

you are every whisper of promise.
when i look at you i hear the laughter of my life,
i remember every dream i have forgotten just after awakening,
i believe in any possibility that i have once touched.

> even when you are not with me,
> you are part of the memories i make.

and now . . . i will be the soil of your rich harvest season.
the season where the pain of the fallow and the burden of
the bountiful come together. i am the orchard in which
you walk and ponder and begin to hear the wind whisper
of the immeasurable breadth of your strengths. i am the
growing places in which you wander and begin to see the
richness of your own knowing. it is in this place where you
may both rest and soar.

———————

in all things & in all your ways . . . may there be wings behind you (angels ever by you). may there be promise before you (vision drawing you onward). may there be hope ever above you (comfort wrapping you in grace). may there be strength beneath you (enthusiasm beyond yourself). and in all times and in all experiences . . . may the colors of your soul rise greatly within you and the light which weaves your soul to greatness will continue to shine and make a clearer way for others.

---

was that you that painted your favorite indigo blue across the sky? no—it was just the dusk greeting the night. at the end of this day i wondered . . . i couldn't help but wonder if this is what you meant when you whispered to me that you would always protect me, even when you couldn't be seen . . . and that everywhere i looked and listened i would see & hear sure signs of your love for me. then . . . it was you . . . wasn't it?

---

love's journey home

love isn't completed as it's returned. it is completed in its
    choice to be given.
love is extended on the force of its existence not because
    it is deserved.
when met with disappointment
love whispers hope.
when confronted with anger
love listens harder.
when faced with challenge
love imagines freely.
when approached with harm
love raises an open palm.
when utterly betrayed
loves knows to walk away tall.
when loved unconditionally
love knows to thrive.
when touched by appreciation and praise
love basks in gratitude.
when shown a new way
love becomes a student.
when walked to a wall
loves finds a way to
continue the journey home.

love is a door

violence erupts, guns kill, bombs drop, new ways of harm
   are strategized:
   still believe in love.
leaders lie, politicians position, large structures serve
   small interests:
   still believe in love.
planet's poisoned, air's choked, creatures weep, imbalances
   create great ills:
   still believe in love.
romance strays, friends fade, family distances, what is familiar
   becomes uncertain:
   still believe in love.
employment changes, plenty vacillates, education waivers,
   questions produce uncertainty:
   still believe in love.
   your efforts will be met with disinterest,
   your generosity will stand with resentment,
   your vision will be discredited and the
   reach of your hand will not be embraced . . .
      still believe in love.
      this great love is not the visit of an unexpected fate
         but rather a
      flame which is kept burning in spite of the winds of harm,
      disappointment, risk, loss, and disloyalty.
         belief in love
         shines in a darkened room.
         it is the single light which illuminates the door—
         the door which opens to the promise of
         a new hope.

*j*udah, my labrador retriever, has taught me a lot about loving. He says,

"It's you, it's you!!!! Oh my, it's you. Let me look at you. Let me touch you. Here. Here. And you scratch my nose! Let me taste you—yep—it's really you and you're the best. Nobody better'n you.

You were gone soooo long!"

"Judah, I only went to the mail box."

"I thought you were gone forever."

I longed on behalf of my sweetest friend, Suze, that she would meet a soul who would adore her, who would love her exactly as she was and see all her remarkable qualities. And—she did meet such a soul. In their company I get to enjoy the ways they risk loving each other. It is a pleasure to observe the languages of love, which are spoken in any walls that contain these two tall hearts. Their loving inspires me and kindles a sense of possibility in me.

jonathan and suze

there are many ways to say
i love you
that require language of a
tall heart, and more than words.
this language can be heard in
the celebration of differences
and the tolerance of other ways,
the easy intimacy shining
from two sleeping faces,
the sweet passing of a long day
spent going nowhere but to each other.

love is a verb in this house in
the most practical of means;
early wakefulness dedicated
to lunch packing,
late conversation against heavy lids and
bedded hands which travel to bodies
of other countries because they cannot
bear remaining in their own;
in the safari of the hours
between dawn and sun down
there are myriad roads
traveled for care of the other
over peculiar purpose to
the singular self.
and while monkey mind could deduce
such assertions are not essential—
    i love you
    is communicated with
    the easy snap of a flag
    unfurled by an
    afternoon wind.

———————

what is the sound of
such a wild heart and
who hears it as well as you?

———————

love walks tall.
never broken, it
breaks all falls.

    travel an uncharted heart.

when i want to see
love defined,
i look at you.

Seize every opportunity to demonstrate your love. If you think a stranger has a beautiful smile as you pass, simply say, "nice smile." What harm could come from speaking loving words? While it's true there's risk in almost everything . . . it becomes a greater risk over time to keep your lovingkindnesses to yourself. There can be no failure in demonstrating love. The success is having the courage to extend love—it has nothing to do with how it is received. Love is full and complete in its giving. Make your own list of what love is, and what it looks like. Remember the most recent time someone told you they loved you . . . reflect on how that made you feel.

fail
with
enthusiasm

intentional change is the most ferocious response to fear.

i am.
you are.
we envision.
there is hope.
possibilities whisper.
in shortfall, there is still abundance. in one expectation which
    was not met there were other presentations of surprise.
let me look you in the eye and say this to you.
i see you.
i recognize in you wonder, enthusiasm, and promise.
i smell the fragrance of possible greatness lingering over your
    shoulder.
i cannot see what you have not done—however, what you
    may accomplish
shines above you like first light. such promise to wear upon
    your head.
let me look you in the eye and ask you, "what do you long
    for? and
will you change the world in some way today?"

———

while the question of life's meaning remains a mystery
i am sure my answer in all instances is YES.

----

marvel that you have grown when you listen to and learn
from a child. recognize tallness of spirit when hurt is
returned with compassion. celebrate creativity as you set
aside the fear of failure. value perspective when, fallen,
there's laughter. see confidence as you glimpse your
own inspired possibility when celebrating the success of
another. the most significant measures of stature are the
ways you choose for yourself.

*a*sk for what you want. Do not assume that you must "make
do" with a second choice. But then, Tony is quick to
point out that the best way to lose is to act as if you have won and
that where ever you are, should be where you *want* to be. Regardless of the where or how you came to be there.

But here's the other side of that line. Do not tolerate unaccept-
able circumstances. Not in the world at large, in the field of your
endeavor, or in a corner of your home. It is not being disagreeable
to make or raise an objection. Many outrageous things take place
due to lack of challenge. Too many. If you object, and determine
it matters, say so. And say so in the most civil and appropriate way
to the context of the situation: in a purposeful and calm voice, in
writing, in a letter, in a raised voice, in a phone call to a television
station.

Conversely . . . let go. Let go of inappropriate, excessive burdens. Let go of worn loyalties, which no longer foster a good exchange or mutual growth. Let go of thoughts or things, which weigh heavily upon your spirit. You make the choice to be present or absent at a place. While certain elements of obligations establish themselves in a structure of community—avoid commitments singularly based upon obligation.

a key to a vital life is an eagerness to learn and a willingness
to change.

lost following a thought, imperiled in a forest of ideas,
overwhelmed by the scent of old books, there is promise
and profound danger waiting in the lines and between the
lines. it is not the words themselves but the thought you
take of the words, which creates the grand adventure. don't
be a tourist; be an adventurer.

---

learning:
is today truly new?
    yes.
do you really leave what has passed behind you?
    yes.
is it in this way that you redeem the pain
and become better, stronger, brighter?
    yes.

The worst kind of prison wall is the one that cannot be
seen. I'm not sure I know anyone who isn't imprisoned
by something—a past that restrains, a current relationship that binds, a sense of limitation that constrains. A remarkable
model for breaking barriers and walking through walls exists for
me in an unlikely place: a medium-security prison.

There I meet with my writing group, many of whom are serving life sentences. I only get to meet with them by advance sched-
uling, presenting my security pass (for which I had to undergo

hours of training) and traveling through two wire fences, a metal detector, five iron doors and past many armed guards. It is behind these barriers where I've been challenged in some of my deepest learning about being free.

Ben Linder: I will remember you.

I twirled the radio dial . . . In 1987 on the upper left edge of the Oregon coast, radio and television signals were capricious. In the early months of running my own business I was looking for something different to keep company with instead of my predictable installment of music. Something to occupy me as I painted each small greeting card by hand. This is the first time I recall listening to national public radio. It was a newscast about an Oregon boy—Ben Linder. The extensive tale that followed was so unlike the zippy news clips I was used to hearing from conventional news reports. The candor of the reporting shocked me.

As the story unfolded I was horrified to learn of the possibility that my own government had complicity in his death. His death while on a mission of compassion as a young engineer. He was working to bring a consistent water source to a small village in Nicaragua.

At the end of the broadcast I was compelled to turn off the radio and sit with my tears. I wrote a poem, which I sent to Ben Linder's family. It was a pledge to a large truth: things are not always as they appear. I must not always believe what my eyes see. One must seek deeper ways of learning many things, which may be true about one thing.

I remember this viscerally. It comes back to me as one of the most significant learning experiences in my life. Ben Linder's death changed the way I gained my information and how I considered the things that I heard. I have kept my promise these many years. I remember Ben Linder . . . and I also remember that things are not always as they seem and your eyes must not determine what you see.

Develop a sharp curiosity. Build upon this skill to observe the world around you and within. Learn from people. All people. Learn from those you do not like. Take some lesson away from difficult events. If you can learn—there is no loss.

Write. Often the best instruction comes from "the pen." The pen has a way of teaching what, at first, appears elusive. Ask hard questions, discover the answers with the pen and quiet. Find solutions, establish and measure goals, find your aspirations, detail your heart.

Make the commitment to learn something that does not come to you easily. Or naturally. This is also a way to walk to the edge of your knowing. It stretches your brain and keeps you smart. Practice. Practice (stop making excuses). Practice that at which you long to excel. Success in your longing requires (you guessed it) practice.

Establish your own inspirational library. Return to these volumes repeatedly for motivation, clarity, comfort, direction. Write your own inspiration piece and place it on the wall. Keep a book and fill it with words that have inspired or heartened you; return to it repeatedly. For centuries this particular practice was called a commonplace book. Maintained over a lifetime you will produce a legacy of significant lessons and pieces of information, which have impacted and formed the life that is uniquely your own.

Recognize and understand your motivation. Give less attention to that which others think and devote the time to discern what you think. Too much concern for the opinions of others is, at the very least, distracting.

appreciate your friends

apparently the angels were quite busy so god sent my friend along.

it is with gratitude that i get to walk with you toward your vision of
excellence, compassionate service, and informed hope.

how long have we known each other?
cannot recount
the we of us
by a clock.

i recognized you
before we met.

i knew you always
when you first. spoke.

tales of your history
were reminders not new:
i grew up
somewhere else
with you.

your destiny that.
my journey this.
threads: warp and woof
defining another kind of beauty
refining utterly other function.

don't recount our ways of knowing
for the who of we two
untangles in the if of
tomorrow
not the is of
yesterday.

an uncommon holiday . . . which celebrates the day we first named
each other "friend."

if you are the question
the answer is yes.
if you are the challenge
the problem is already solved.
then and now
yesterday and tomorrow
i go on choosing you.

My friend, Rachael, wrote as my Christmas present her intention that we should pass a lovely leather bound journal back and forth over many years. She explained it this way: To one of my very favorite people—to share our thoughts and inspirations through this crazy journey of life. "Crazy journey." She must not have heard that George Carlin calls it a freak show.

After lots of Shel Silverstein and Robert Frost she finished with a flourish of these words:

Do you know how wonderful you are? Your laugh that fills a room, your creative energy, your loving heart. Thank you for making my every day a little more extraordinary.

Christmas night I wrote back to her in that leather book:

I cried as I held this book in my hand. A gift born of talent, tenderness, and mutuality. It would only make sense to you, Rachael, that a little over twenty years ago I gave such gifts to my friends for Christmas. Puzzled recipients, all.

But this recipient received the gift with grace and certainty. Grace to be embraced by such molten talent along with an enormously gifted family and certainty that here is a friend to whom I would hand the rope, on belay, in order to climb the mountain.

And what a mountain we will climb.

It is not that we have the same heart beating within us. No. Not that. We have, however, been both burned and warmed by the same flames.

While our extraction varies, it is from the same well that we draw our water to drink and to feed our gardens.

It is not our shared pulse, for our pulse and breath come differently. It is our common path and shared elements that bind us like sisters. Two mountains sharing a valley.

Months passed and we both had reason to consider our goals and that for which we were each longing. Rachael returned the leather book to me having written:

"In the long run, men hit only what they aim at."

          —H. D. Thoreau

These words ring in my ears as I sit here listening to Thoreau (on tape). The importance of knowing what you truly want, and striving for it. But focusing only on a target, don't you also risk missing the incredible experiences and opportunities that you never knew you could have? The glorious tangents, the meandering pathways that might lead to something beyond our wishes? Even in failure, do we not find often that our vision and resolve are strengthened? Perhaps what is more important than hitting exactly what you are aiming at is the simple act of aiming, in itself. To actively move in the direction of your dreams and be open to the voice of the universe. To pursue each promising lead and allow the story to unfold. But considering our daily lives, it is a struggle for most of us to build up any kind of momentum at all. We find ourselves idling in what we think are pressing tasks. There is something to be said for stability and consistency, but I believe that if you do not make room in your life for purpose and passion, there will never be any. And so, then, you can only hit what you aim at. Say, where'd I put those gym shoes?

I wrote back to her:

"Something beyond our wishes . . . "

Tony Kesler has said many things to me over the years. Perhaps the most consistent message has been: Want what you have. Want to be where you are.

Aphorism has flown regarding the longings of our lives.

> *"Be the peace you wish to see in the world."*
> —*Gandhi*
> *"If you can dream it, you can achieve it."*
> —*William Arthur Ward*

But as this day dawns I echo the questions I asked my same-birthday friend, Jonathan: "What if this is the life of which

I've dreamed? What if it's true that, as the despair.com *funny folks suggest, the main purpose of my life is that my mistakes should serve as a warning to others?"*

These questions suggest two things to me. If I am dissatisfied with the where of where I stand and the what of what I do, I can either:

a) change the dreams I'm dreaming or

b) love the life I'm living and live it knowing it is everything I need.

Perhaps this is one of the keys to understanding, in practical application, the suggestion to live as if this is all there is.

I might answer the question, "If this were your last day alive, what would you do?" with a list of frenetic activities producing a wishfest of fingers brushing unfilled dreams. But on my finest, most grounded day I know I would answer this way:

I would walk around beauty and I would express my gratitude to my friends. Acting in my gift and being grateful for the highest gifts of my life is as good as it gets. And that makes it the best day, even if it (is) (might be) the last day.

So! Let me practice and tell you I am grateful in the small for your loving care of my dog, the tender respect of my domicile, the miles you've traveled to make my life and travels more seamless. In the large I am grateful for your wandering ways, the way of seeing you have, which sheds light in a place that is mostly dark. I am blessed to stand in your gracious and wise company and am schooled by the many ways you live out your friendship.

Value diversity among your friends. You each contribute in different ways to the lives of the others. Do things willingly. Not because of the appeal of the specific things but because you act from caring for your friend. Do not assume that your friend will, or needs to, hold the same views as you. Do not assume your friend will change in any way—give your love as is. Change is a welcome thing but not an expected thing. And also . . . provide the free field for your friend to change. Do not hold your friend's sail to one place. Celebrate change and growth even if you are unable to change and grow in the same direction as your friend. Rivers part at a fork . . . and sometimes, so do friends. That just means there are two ways for others to travel behind, not just one.

Write thank-you notes. (Ah, here is where obligation wins.) Take time to honor the thought behind the generosity of your friend. This means not a fax, not a phone call, not an e-mail but your flesh pushing a pen on paper, addressing it, and posting it promptly.

When you have a positive observation about someone (even a stranger), tell them. This keeps you from the "I wish I had said . . ." later on.

Ask your friends for help when you need it. And give it when you're asked.

A gift can be given without an occasion. "Grateful that you are my friend" is occasion enough.

*how do i choose to spend the currency of myself? the currency of
my being. my energy is the most profound fiscal instrument. in what,
in whom, will i invest today?*

t's very straightforward—I do what I choose. If I am doing it,
I choose to do it. I am my own captain. No one makes me
go to work, clean my house, make a call. And that frustrated
explanation my girlfriends offer me after a weekend away from
work: "I had to watch football." No. Nope. You chose to watch
football. You could have spent yourself in any way. You choose.
You're in charge.

A client, a Methodist minister, came in one Monday morning.
She'd given one of the most memorable children's sermons in her
career the day before. She was talking to the children about how
all things work together for those who love God. And she used
the phrase, "When life gives you lemons, make lemonade." One
young man was adamant in his preferences. And the third time
he insisted on his version . . . she adjusted her sermon. The young
man's wisdom?

"When life gives you lemons, make hot chocolate." He
explained that he did not like lemonade.

So from the most difficult of circumstances, we can build something of our own choice. Just because a thing is handed to me does
not mean it must be grasped by my hand.

In discussing a variety of options around a single action I often
remind myself that the foremost function of a plan is that it should
be modified and not simply followed.

what it's like to confront regret
you are my colorful history
you blow across my walking
like a hot summer night wind.
even in this way i burn for you
when i breathe.

you are my longing history
i stand in the field of my choices
and see the results of my effort grow about me.
i would not choose you if you
    stood before me now.
i would not.
i would not reach for the skin
that made me strike lightening.
i would not touch the lips
whose laughter brightened my sober soul.
i would not wrap myself around
the passion which inspired me
to imagine new ways to love you.
i would not.
because once i did and it almost
cost me everything.
you are my vicious history.
i carry you in this safe way:
i carry you in the echoes of my music.

it is there your vibrant soul
falls into my arms and
that is how i hold you
my sweet, my unchosen history.

in my music
your history sings itself into my every day.
and, on this, my ordinary every day,
i do not trade my memories of you then
for the reality of your now. i am
content to hum to your lyrics and walk on.

So as I consider the cost of carrying regret I say to myself, move on
in a different way. Do not let regret over paths not chosen travel
with you. Walk gently in each of your days, set aside remorse and
willfully direct your longing.

Resist the draw of retaliation. Defy the urge to bring harm
to another because harm has been brought to you. Make a
decision and then set about it with conviction. Analyze and
ponder to a point. Recognize when this process becomes
circular rather than productive. Avoid obsessiveness over issues
and particular hurts. Choose items in your environment based
on the value, meaning, and function they hold. Do not allow
obligation to bind you to physical things.

may your heart and the hearts of those you love be awakened to all
their dreams.

may this be the place from which you launch your dreams.
may this be the castle from which you go forth and
conquer and return to celebrate and rest. may this be the
dance at which you learn to craft a confidence and ease.
in these rooms may you discover the tools to build your
vision—or may you have the grace to seek that which you
need so your spirit may soar. may you always know your
family as your safe and good home.

i love it when we are together and a stranger says to us, "wow! you
must be related." we just smile, don't we?

Understanding comes upon us at odd times. I realized only a
few years ago that my mother's most loving gesture was to
get me an adult library card, not a juvenile card, when I was seven.
The more calloused view would be that she didn't want to have to
come and sign out the non-juvenile books that I was always picking out. Nope. People show love in the ways that they are able.
And in this way, a profound way, really, my mother gifted me with
a world of words restrained only by four walls and posted hours
of operation.

My friend Len asked me if the man who raised me was a "dad"
or a "father." I answered in this way:

He was a dad when he started doing "Increase your word
power" with me when I was four.

He was a dad when he explained management issues to me when I was eight.

He was a dad when he made me wait in the car while he had "one more" (and made sure I had a book for the "one more" after the one more . . . I'm quite a reader).

He was a dad when he taught me first aid and used me and my skills to offer roadside assistance at any accident.

He was a dad the day we wept as we watched Richard Nixon resign and knew America had lost something of its pride that day.

He was a dad all through my twenties when I needed advice and was far away.

He was a dad when he remembered he had Alzheimer's and told me it was a hellava thing to lose your mind a tolerance point at a time.

The day he died in my arms, he was my father.

Create a family circle of your own. It may consist of persons to whom you are related and some (or all) to whom you are not. You choose. This is the circle of family with whom you can celebrate, with whom you can enjoy acceptance and safety.

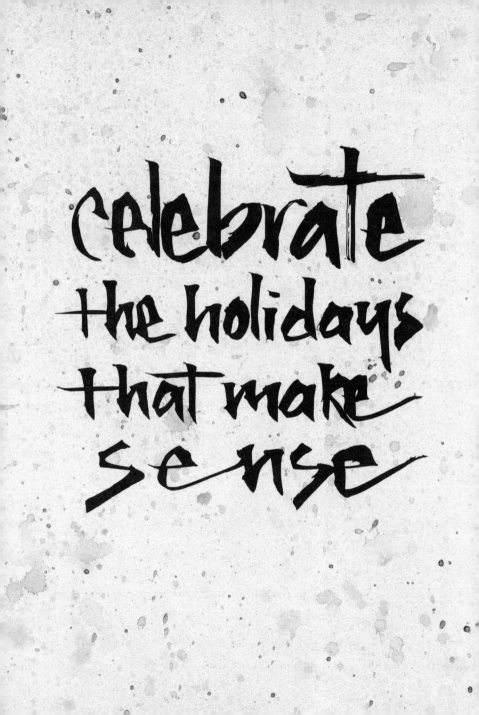

. . . and celebrate them in the way that makes sense to you.

people like my kite as long as it flies with their wind.

as the moon wraps the end
of our day
we sit with the consequences
of our intentions
and pour a warm cup of gratitude
for our family, our friends.
with such grace
we prepare for another day.

Some days are simply holidays to replenish the currency of your spirit. My currency is replenished in beauty and solitude and genuine intimacy.

By beauty I mean the beauty of a well-crafted story, an elegant environment, the glorious sunset over the bird refuge with the glimmer of the Willamette River sparkling like a single diamond at the neck of a grand dame, the beauty of human kindness and compassionate acts, and the beauty of seeing what seems invisible.

By solitude I mean time alone, in quiet, with no noise save the noise of the natural breathing, which comes from a contented Earth. By solitude I mean perhaps driving an hour away and secreting myself in a little spot and being anonymous and having a breakfast of croissant and coffee and reading an outdated copy of *Harper's* and having no where to go and no one to see.

By genuine intimacy I mean—well, this. Telling the truth to another human being for no reason other than they asked for the truth, having friends that I can awaken to with an unpainted face, sharing the trust that comes in time after you've had the chance to forgive each other's errors and celebrate each other's successes.

Spend your various holidays in ways that are significant to you. If the way you traditionally spend a holiday causes you trauma—change it. Create a new celebration or adjust the manner in which you relate to the old one. Choose and celebrate your own traditions. Pack them away and bring them out again and again. Introduce them to others and celebrate them over and over again.

Lead

or follow a

Leader

possibilities. skeletal possibilities, sewn by the threads of
change, have the nerve to stand in the wind and sing,
stand in a crowd and shout, stand before masses and lead.
and then they, these loosely held potentials, sit in the dark,
light a candle, and craft the day, which tomorrow will
paint.

---

remember & know . . . what is my vision? i remember. i
will paint it. what are my goals? i remember. i will dance
them. where is my integrity? i know. i will build upon
it. where is my personal responsibility? i know. i will
appropriately extend it. at every turn, in each opportunity
i will stand tall & fully myself.

---

you walk people to places they never imagined they would
stand. you stand with them. you walk people to places they
hoped to go—but could not conceive the way. once there,
you stand with them and broaden their view even more.
you are an excellent vehicle. an inviter: one who draws
from before and entices; one who coaches from behind
and inspires. shoulder to shoulder you extend camaraderie,
deep humor, and shared vision. what pleasure—to march
in a parade, which shall always be remembered as you.

Fortunately for me I've had friends in my life who have been strong leaders, mentors. In the earlier decades of my life Sally Steidel mentored me by patiently and endlessly listening to my stories, observations, complaints, and wonderings. She pronounced to me one day, one memorable day, that all these experiences and explorations of my life would come to be recounted in a remarkable book. I may have laughed when she said it those many years ago. But she did not. As leaders do, she saw something in me I could not then see in myself.

In the shallowness of celebrity-based culture, leaders can be found. Consider Lewis Lapham of *Harper's* magazine, whose historian spirit has roared the truth for years. Think of Al Gore, who has consistently told an "inconvenient truth," president Bill Clinton, who is following two terms as president with global service, senator Hillary Rodham Clinton, who is the epitome of lifelong learning, Tom Cruise, Mary Oliver, Howard Zinn, Shel Silverstein. While I've been blessed to meet a few of these folks, thankfully I don't have to know tall spirits personally for their leadership qualities to impact my vision and ways. It is with leaders such as these that I want to fill my dance card at the Possibility Ball. (Who are the leaders of your life?)

A leader/mentor in my life that I am fortunate to actually know is Tony Kesler, joined by the unique coaching team of his family: Tina who teaches me the duck-like quality of allowing things to roll off my feathers and models a laughter that fills the darkest corner of a day with levity and promise, Anthony, whose discipline in learning has been an inspiration to me since he was ten, and Taylina, who regularly mines the vastness of my heart and invites me to play.

Conversation and asking questions are core to Tony's leadership. (Interestingly, Byron Katie in her book *Loving What Is* patterns a construct of effective questioning that Tony has intuitively followed most of his life.)

He can travel anywhere or do anything in the vehicle of words. The number of times he's said, "It's not about where we *are*, it's about where we *could* be" exceeds my recollection. And I'm pretty sure I lifted the phrase, "Set aside the is to discover the if" many years ago. But he lifted Taylina's quote, "I remember once, when I was older . . ." So I figure it all comes out in the cosmic wash.

A lengthy conversation remains vivid although it was years ago. When discussing a draft piece of my production writing, the concept of metaphysical walls was introduced. At the time, I believed I was relatively unencumbered by expectation, that I lacked restrictions in my ways of seeing.

Without demonstrating judgment and asserting no sense of condescension, Tony began identifying parameters, which he'd observed me setting about my life. (Gasp, walls!) I registered surprise. He suggested that because my writing and philosophies enable others to step outside boundary and live beyond the wall of expectation, I persuaded myself that I lived that way as well.

He identified and began to explode neat packages of concept, dependable definitions, and orderly borders, which I'd insidiously placed around the lands of my life to contain my days and safely store my spirit.

I considered his observations and saw the truth in them. He delivered an interesting challenge. What I remember of it distills to this: What if you walk through walls? Inspire yourself as you inspire so many others. Surely the borders that surround your soul are marked differently. Travel across them and begin your fearless journey of discovery of how far you can walk when you choose to not just write about it but to actually walk through walls.

I continue to walk through walls. And though I sometimes step on their toes on my way, characteristic of good friends, this family overlooks my shortcomings and are somewhere along the road, celebrating with me or cheering me on.

Living in an age with access to so much information, I am boundless, almost, in my access to information about leaders all over the globe. And leadership that spans time. I turn often to the time when America was choosing its own way to find patterns of leadership. Reading biographies has been a lifelong way for me to select qualities and styles of management, leadership, and being. In coming to understand the views and motivations of seminal participants in our own country, I come close to the heroic and am inspired. Howard Zinn, a modern patriot and agent of change, inspires me to lean toward my own heroics. He asserts in *Declarations of Independence: Cross-examining American Ideology,* "To depend . . . on authorities and experts is . . . a violation of the spirit of democracy. . . . Important decisions of society are within the capability of ordinary citizens."

the hero who stands closest to you
stand tall america
come to understand
the greatest strengths of
this country are
held in the hearts of
ordinary citizens.

stand forward america
reach to the hand
of the leaders who have walked
before you and continue
in the ways of their legacy.

stand fast america
hold firmly to your own vision
embrace the depth of your intentions and
pour them into the cup
of your days in vision,
in service to a common good.

see clearly america
the vision and the possibility before you
in a world that is trembled, remain unshaken: inspired by the
    great heart of those who
walk ahead of you
look in the mirror and catch a glimpse of
the hero who stands closest to you.

As I studied President Clinton's words for hours, looking for quotes
to letter artfully on work in his museum store, I came to a core
understanding of how he has maintained his circle of friends for so
many decades. "Helping another realize their dream is the surest
step toward realizing your own." Since Bill Clinton was a child,
with clarity about his own dreams, he made at least as much time
available to promote and support the realization of the dreams of
his friends. And those would be many of the same friends who
stand at his side these decades later.

listening to bill clinton i observe . . .
an amazing patience is required to be footed and
fully present in the arena of an ordinary moment.
and perhaps the real view is
there are no ordinary moments for an
extraordinary person. every moment is an
unopened possibility to which the visionary
applies a unique set of tools.
ask yourself "have you been caught in the act today?"
caught in the act of caring
    leading
    teaching
    innovating
    inspiring others
    healing?

Connie fails, the curator for the President Clinton Museum Store in Little Rock, Arkansas, likes to tell the story of the reporter who assertively sidled up to her and insisted that he immediately speak to "the person in charge here." Connie smiled and replied, "I am the person in charge here. You can tell because I'm the one with a broom in my hand."

I like to call that leader with a broom in her hand, Connie the Conduit. She has an almost supernatural ability to connect people to create a new thing, a remarkable synergy. She assured me I had to meet Paul Leopoulos and his family. She said she sensed it was really important. She made sure we got to meet. The Leopoulos family founded *theafoundation.org* following the death of their vivacious and dynamic teenaged daughter, Thea. As a way of redeeming the wrenching loss to their family they leaned forward in their grief and chose to reach out to other young people by introducing the arts into their lives. The arts had been a real key to confidence in Thea's life and they wanted to pass that gift of confidence on. In finding a way to grow in and through their grief the Leopoulos family enliven and inspire hundreds of young people throughout the state of Arkansas. They dream of taking the program nationally. This is leadership, which rises up from the heart and stands tall. This is the phoenix fire taking loss and making it legacy. This is leadership that leans.

From early in my childhood I heard my father recount a story, which typified his management and leadership style. The building in which he was a graveyard-shift foreman had sheet metal for a roof. It was a good thing in the hot summer, somehow serving to help cool the building. In the winter, however, it was a liability. The snow piled and worked to invert the sheet metal, causing serious concern about a roof collapse. The roof had to be cleared of its snow. It was a dangerous job. Climbing a ladder to a warehouse roof in a snow storm to shovel snow off sheet metal wasn't anyone's idea of a good time. But it was necessary for everyone's safety that four people subject themselves to this danger. All were grateful that Oregon was not long subjected to seasonal snow storms.

In advance of the effort my father did two things. He placed enough equipment and outdoor gear for four people in the corner by the door. Then, when it was time he left his desk, went to the corner, and started suiting up. He assured me, each time he told me the story, that he was willing to go on the roof and get the job done alone. Although he never had to do the job by himself. He was always joined by three other men. Each time, it was a different group, but by the time my dad was suited up and put his hand to one of the four snow shovels, there were three men in line behind, ready to grab the other shovels.

When I was older he elaborated on the story just a little. He explained to me why he would never accept offered promotions into management, off the production-facility floor.

In a suit, you tell four men that they have to climb on the roof and put themselves at risk for the greater good. On the production floor, you climb on the roof for the greater good, putting yourself at risk, and there are people who follow. Not because you told them to, but because you led the way.

In the first couple of years of operating my own business, I kept a shovel in the corner of the space in which I worked to remind me of the kind of leader I wanted to be.

what is a voice
    if it does not
    raise against injustice?

what is a voice
    if it does not
    sing for change?

what is a voice
    if it does not
    speak for those who cannot?

what is a voice
	if it refrains from
	forming the hearts vision?

what is a voice
	if it merely
	mimics the machination of culture?

a stilled voice is a
	dried reed,
		lost toy,
			torn page . . .
	a broken feather
		floating down an
			emptied canyon.

what is a voice
	if it remains silent
	against leagues of tyranny?

Demonstrate leadership in an unconventional way. Raise your hand. Raise your voice. Write a letter. Lead yourself—the parade begins with you.

yes, we change.
yet our love and commitment
is the bridge which walks us
each between our growing visions.

———————

walk through walls.
allow no limitations to be defined on your behalf:
choose your own borders
(if you choose borders)
walk through walls
(if there are any walls)
sing with resonance:
we change. we move on.

———————

if there is joy in the labor of the hands . . . it is more than
simply "work." if there is value in the difficult experience
. . . it becomes more than just "loss." if there is enthusiasm
at the beginning of the day . . . it is not just "ordinary." we
lift ourselves up on the wings of our own vision and hope.

———————

live boldly. laugh loudly. love truly. play as often as you can. work as smart as you are able. share your heart as deeply as you can reach. as you awaken may your dreams greet you by name and may you answer, "yes!" as you walk may angels gather at your shoulder and may you know they stand with you. as you rest may all your endeavors be rooted in contentment and peace.

erendipity walked a young woman named Gina Bramucci into my employ for a summer when she was seventeen. When Gina returned to work with me for a second summer, she also stayed in my home. We had many occasions to discuss our dreams and ideals for our lives. She asserted that she wanted to travel to Italy but was dismayed that it would be years before she could afford to do that. We started questioning that assumption together. One evening we worked some amazing math. The results were: we agreed to purposely withhold certain expenditures in our everyday experience—brew coffee or take a thermos instead of purchasing a prepared coffee drink, make a lunch in advance rather than expending the funds for a prepared meal—and dedicate those saved funds to a travel account. We assessed that we would be able to travel to Italy the following spring. And we did.

In the course of that journey we were on a night train headed for Siena. Siena . . . where Gina was destined to spend a study-year abroad. Against the measured orchestration of the tracks beneath us I asked Gina to tell me what she longed to do: "When someone asks you what you do for a living, what do you want to be able to say?"

Tentatively, amid explanations of why it seemed unlikely and punctuated with the advice of well-intended people in her world who pointed out that there's not much of a lucrative future in what she wanted to do, she managed to answer that she wanted to be able to say, "I am a writer."

Over the years it has been my joy to periodically ask Gina, "Hey . . . what do you do for a living?" With a master's degree in journalism, I was reasonably confident in the answer she was going to provide me.

"I am a writer." I'm delighted with her answer. Frequently her humanitarian aide work takes precedence over writing. If I were to ask her today she'd tell me she provides medical care to displaced Sudanese elders and children, that she guides volunteer eye doctors to the various camps to facilitate them offering their services. But here's the key. If I asked her, "Are you doing what you love?" Her answer would be, without reservation, "Yes." It takes perseverance and courage to do what you love. And a willingness, at times, to step away from what is safe and predictable.

If Mae and Bette were correct and growing old isn't for wimps, then neither is owning your own business. I do what I love. In doing what I love I get to do some things that, well, I barely like. But I place them in the whole of choosing my own labor and love them for the place they hold in the whole. Some decisions that I face in the machinations of enterprise make me grind my teeth. I place those things, as well, in the context of my vision and my love for my work. I have worked for others. And in those labors I have chosen to celebrate the presence of the things that I have loved and tried, then as now, to take the tasks, which don't exactly make my heart sing, and place them in the context of my bigger picture.

Value the work of your hands and the workings of your mind. Find employment (that thing to which you choose to apply the labor of your hands and the movements of your mind in exchange for pay) that provides satisfaction and meaning. Your endeavor should return to you a high measure of pleasure for the effort you invest.

Performing work without meaning brings frustration and a peculiar brittleness. Find work, or elements of your work, which challenge and satisfy. If this is not possible, start to dream of work that will fulfill your heart and hands.

Create memories. Don't just get splattered with the paint of pain . . . grab a brush and create a masterpiece. Create memories that will enhance your days merely by reflecting on them.

When I spoke of my friends, Brad and Craig, to others, I called them the two that came in when everybody else was going out. Beyond reasonable explanation Brad and Craig always happened to "be around" when my battery needed charging, when an over-medicated driver crashed through the front of my store, when I faced unusual challenges in the life of my business. The phrase "they show up" applied to these two men, start to finish.

So, a fast-track lymphatic cancer seemed the least likely thing that would come up on Brad's road. His vivacious, larger-than-life road. But it did. Walking his loss with Craig and Brad's mom and those who adored him at varying degrees creates a story, which underscores the need to live as if this is all there is. I wrote these pieces over the six weeks (that felt like six years) of his journey into dying.

> *The MASH theme song has always been wrong. Suicide is not painless. There's the preamble that's painful and there's the trail of pain left behind. Death from cancer just has a different set of wails, different whys. The why of cancer cries in my bones, the worry of cancer so close to my own home shudders me (this only happens to friends and relatives of other people . . .). Surely Frankie taught me that's not true. Death knocks upon doors with the appearance of malicious arbitrariness. Upon reflection it is neither malicious nor arbitrary (am I willing to believe in a plan?). So many of our life consequences are the result of our own actions.*
>
> *Am I willing to believe . . . ? I ask myself this in so many different ways. For a great misfortune cast over another's life naturally invites introspection upon my own. How selfish we*

are with someone else's breath. The tears I wept were not for Brad not breathing; they were for me not seeing Brad breathe. The grief of loss is so utterly self-centered. If it were not, I could perhaps be more philosophically indigenous and ask death what my job is in Brad's journey, focus on my many gratitudes. Perhaps my lesson in this is how to learn to lean forward into a death. Leaning forward into Brad's death gives it a grace rather than a sense of side-show, eleventh-hour, miracle-snake-oil, "I'll pray and promise to give up certain activities if you'll save him" bartering. Grace rather than negotiation.

my fancy dancing boy
mischief eyes laughing and
daring me to go ahead—take myself
    s o s e r i o u s l y.
my fancy dancing boy
gifted story teller inviting
laughter from all listening ears.

    where is the music today
    my dear boy
    and what gamble shall
    we lay our money
    down upon today, dear boy

no music.
no money.
no day, you say?

my fancy dancing boy
who is it who shall know me
like the last chapter of a best
book and know my music
like familiar notes of a
first learned piano piece?

(and how is it come to be your cancer
becomes questions of my loss. let
me pause in my own losing to see your
losing. it is twice the pain. but that is
what friends do, isn't it? friends see
twice, feel twice. live twice. once for
ourselves and once for the heart we
hold close. and I wonder, then,
does that mean, I die twice?)

my boy. my dear boy.
i strenuously object to this idea of dying.
can we not make other plans?

A medical team made a Herculean effort to invite Brad to recover. It was a drive through the Italian alps at top speed. Up . . . down . . . in a dark tunnel, blinding light, up, down. Recovery long but arduous. Recovery. Not likely. We'll try this—it worked, it didn't work. In all the sincere reach for Brad's distant healing, we all suspected the end of the song. No one was willing to sing it.

For you, Craig.

called home through winter
how i weary of this winter
its cold song too deep to sing.
can we not wrap ourselves in daffodils
and dance a simple jig with spring?

three seasons grace my calendar
the year is sliced in three . . .
between autumn and this finer grace
a dying sits before you and me.

this stillness, this labored whisper
comes painfully and long.
trusted hearts know our truest wish for
our friend—is to know his final dawn.

how I weary of this winter
it's memories already harsh and steep.
the sweetness of this passing breath
dispel the harm: kindnesses keep.

how i weary of this winter
such pain—soon may it slide
from this season of travail:
in his own spring he can abide.

our shared season of green-ness growing
will come quickly, with a prayer,
and pass in the way as his winter moves
and in grace, dwells in safety, there.

even in this wearied winter my friends'
eyes speak a peace, all the same.
i know the angels have heard the answer
when our friend called—
for god always answers to his name.

The last time I saw my friend, his eyes were remarkably bright at seeing me. Gasping back tears as I rested my hand lightly on his chest, which was heaving with labored breathing, he opened his eyes and asked me if I was okay. Oh, the irony sticks with me. He managed several words. I only could understand three of them: "I love you." And regardless of the sound of any of his words, that's what my friend Brad always meant when he spoke with me.

be avid. create apart from perfection. risk failure. cover
your words with sweat. run a little. excruciatingly
touch. laugh until you cry. dance with your eyes closed.
understand you die a little every day . . . be enlivened.

Abdurrashid, a member of my prison-based writing group, thanked me for asking him Mary Oliver's question. That question asking what we might choose for our one wild life, which is so precious. In coming to that question he freed himself to dream of changing some small part of the world for good. I shared these thoughts with him:

> I wonder if nearly every person doesn't dream of changing the world or some part of the world. As a writer, some large inimitable motivation has to press my pen into action. I remember delivering speeches to my dog, as a child. Grand plans. Magnificent hopes for the world. Now, here's the red-faced truth. I (still) deliver speeches to the dog that now looks after and herds me. Yep. Full-blown speeches. And I'll be, if he doesn't look patiently appreciative of the effort.
>
> Many poets have asked us what we will do with our precious lives. Not the precious life that starts when I lose weight, get stronger, make more money, change jobs, get outta here—no. This life. This one extraordinary, unfettered, improbable, never-to-be-repeated-in-a-breath-just-like-this-one, wild and precious life.
>
> It means now. When? Not now; maybe later, you think. No! One life. This one. This now. This choice. This unlazy, enlivened, awakened moment in which all you are and all you know meets in a confluence and produces a decision. Not always an action, but always a decision. To continually defer is to progressively and increasingly atrophy, whither, die.
>
> What is it you will do with your one wild, not-to-be-repeated life?

Is there time for bitterness, for smallness? (Thanks, Richard Nixon, for this piece of advice: "Never be petty.") Is there time for succumbing to whispers, to fear? Of course not.

It's wild. It's precious. It's your life. Nurture. Fend. Respect. Embrace and for the sake of all we hold holy, live it!

It's easy to die. Living's the challenge.

When you reach for something out of habit ask yourself, "How would I like to remember this moment?" Do one thing differently each day. Just to see how it goes. Have the courage to speak words to someone you encounter assuming you would never see them again.

lean
forward
into your
life

or.
reminders

I WILL *never* FORGET THIS EXPERIENCE. THIS LESSON IS learned and will stay with me.

The severity of an experience seems to sear the lesson of it into my consciousness. Indelibly making it a part of my being. And yet, as it happens along into life, the burn of knowing was not burned so deeply as I thought. Quizzically I ponder, "How is it that this thing which I thought I had learned so well, I apparently did not learn at all? For here again am I—as they say—same song, *seventeenth* verse.

This question led me to turn to the alphabetical tab *R* in my planning book. *R* for reminders. I pledged to begin myself a list of reminders. At the moment when I was certain I had learned a thing so well I would never ever need a lesson of it again, I purposed to record it. Just in case. A set of crib notes for the grand examination of my life. A little cheat sheet that might give me the foot up I needed at a moment when I experienced quiz brain freeze and all the hard knowledge, which easily traveled with me when I didn't need it, suddenly froze up and dropped out of my brain at the instant I needed it most.

Reminders. For if a lesson is true in one context of my life, could it not be true in another? Broadly applied? I asked that question and the answer was resoundingly yes. First I had to remember.

I kept this list for several years during a time of experiences completely unfamiliar to me. Although in this time I was a writer of aphorisms and a word artist of any number of "posters" with my sayings lettered upon them, I had no idea that I was building a piece of writing, lesson by lesson. However, when I came to the bottom of the tattered page in my planning book, it was apparent that I had inadvertently written a companion piece to "Live with Intention." The side note to myself would have read something like this, "While you endeavor to follow the components of "live with intention" in each of your days, let these reminders help you learn to apply those aspirations more successfully." And they have.

most of the things which seem so significant aren't.
don't take it personally—it's not usually about you.
pay attention. know when to leave. curiosity takes courage.
the most important promises are the ones you make to
yourself. appreciation lasts longer than complaint.
being nice isn't always best. surprise is as powerful as
consistency. listen to your inclination. there's a
difference between protecting yourself and
defending yourself. your eyes must
not determine what you see.
play more.
stand tall.
imagine.

most of the
things which
seem so
significant
aren't

My list of gratitudes, were I to pen it, would consist wholly of people and experiences, not a single thing. The experiences of performance and travel and writing, which have invigorated me and teaching, which has moved me, and conversations and sights, which have challenged and changed me. The people and creatures of my life.

It can only be called a sadness that so much of our collective life's currency is spent in the acquisition of things and then consumed by the placement, presentation, preservation, and protection of those things. Ethos. Compassion. The love of our friends and family. The greater good over the smaller struggle. That's what we wear to the grave. I have lived mired in things, and not. I prefer the not.

George Carlin was on *Dennis Miller Live*. "How do you live with the brilliance and cynicism without going crazy?" Dennis asked him. With his characteristic enigmatic smile, Carlin responded, "Look. When you're born you're given a ticket to a freak show. Sit back and enjoy the entertainment."

Teasingly I told the first group of eighteen medium-security inmates in my journal writing class that it took me over three years to break in to their prison. Following the laughter I asked how long it took them to break in to these walls. One particularly attentive participant took my question as literal, not rhetorical, and answered, "A youth of poor judgment and one moment of an irrevocably bad choice." That answer came from Terry Zion.

Years earlier, when confronted with the walls with which many of my regular class participants imprisoned themselves, I began wondering if it might actually be easier to teach people who were literally in prison. The thought stayed with me and through a series of circumstances, my company came to be affiliated in a professional manner with a medium-security men's prison in Salem,

Oregon. For several years I made inquiries, submitted proposals, and talked to various managers within the institution. Position changes and ever-increasing priorities measured against a shrinking budget caused my inquiry to remain unanswered.

One day a professional associate was giving me a tour of not only the whole department with which I had business, but the entire facility. An office caught my attention. It was filled with color. Positive sayings. Photographs. It was the only spot in the entire facility that actually looked like any fun. I asked my guide whose office it was.

He told me it belonged to the Transition Services Coordinator, Fay Gentle. I told him I'd like to meet her. That I was confident that she was the person who would help me realize my vision of teaching inmates the various benefits of journal keeping.

He gave me her number. I called. Three weeks later I taught my first class and met Terry Zion. Terry was around my age, I thought. Earnest. Eager to listen and willing to learn what I had to share. Terry struck me as a rich book just waiting to be opened by somebody who knew how to read that particular language. The language of potential.

In four sessions it was apparent to me that Mr. Zion was a talented writer and had a lot to say. As we parted company for what I thought would be the last time, I laid my hand on his shoulder and emphatically said, "You keep writing."

With certainty he assured me, "I will."

Even in this I learned that what seems so significant, isn't. I went into that place thinking I was going to teach. I walked out understanding that I was there to learn. Terry articulates his sense of this lesson in a piece he's written called, "Grace."

A distant hand controls the light in my cell, illuminating my world at precisely those times when I would rather lie in darkness. The interruption places me between a destructive past and a monotonous future, roused from a slumber that pretends to be peace. Yesterday's guilt is kindled anew as justice carries the deeds of the past. The temptation is to hide under the blanket, to go back to that time when sleep was the answer.

Awakened, my mind goes to that place where memories live as stories that never end the way they should. Bygones drift suspended in the grief of hindsight, forever wondering how things could be different. Hope and fantasy then make their intrusion, striving for something other than the here and now. Routine prevents my escape.

Cursing the light, my companions stir with me, uncovering the lie that we could hide here forever. A communal voice rises among us, mocking the day with a mixture of defiance and depression. The air is its own blanket, covering me with the smells and frustrations of other men. Yesterday is gone; its lessons remain.

Our confinement testifies to that time when we surrendered our dreams to our passions, forgetting that there is a difference. Now, those dreams and passions are forever the same: lost. Lost like the dreams and passions of our victims. Again, there is a difference. Ours were wasted: theirs were stolen. The light persists.

Hope and fantasy return anew and they are not the same. Fantasy tempts me to hide in slumber and the quiet of darkness. Hope draws me onward, carrying the lessons of the past in the work of today. The choices are equal burdens, though one seems heavier than the other. The temptation again is to lie in the darkness, pretending that there is nothing to do.

My neighbor reads pictures of women as stories because words on the page seem foreign to him. His neighbor sees people in colors of hatred, fearing the likeness in the face of our sin. The man in the box at the end of the cellblock laughs with the demons who visit his sleep. Some people around me see love as passion, not knowing that sacrifice more resembles the truth. I examine myself as I lie here among them, afraid that not knowing applies to me too.

People come and go from these illuminated boxes, and each of them responds to the light in their own way. Some ignore it and some are driven to madness. I cannot explain the difference. Nor can I understand why the light keeps me from madness, yet refuses to allow me the peace of forgetting. A kind of wisdom tells me that I should pay attention. Sleep and rest become two different things.

Rest comes when I ask God for forgiveness, driven there by that incessant light. It is there I watch and pray. It is there that I understand that forgiving is not forgetting, or pretending that nothing has happened. Grace tells me that I may continue while those I have harmed no longer breathe the hope of tomorrow. The light tells me that it is time to get out of bed, and long past time for ignoring the work of today.

After working for many years with Terry and a fine group of talented writers in that institution, I came to a hard perspective on the nature of grace and justice. A remarkable man, a former high school English teacher, willingly took over my role in the writing group. He asked these inmates, with whom he had written and worked for months, a difficult question. He asked them where was the justice in their incarceration. He asserted they were more given to the greater good, more committed to personal growth and integrity than most people he knew on the outside. I remember Terry answered his earnest question in this way, "I took something, which I had no right to take. And in that taking, I can never give it back. I have been imprisoned. And over many years I have grown into a responsible and reasonable man. I have come to understand my crime and have turned my life around. It is only after that point, after that turn around, that justice begins to be extracted. And so I'm here—giving back from my own life, in small part, what can never be given from the life I took."

One day, as Fay and I were discussing the various benefits and outcomes of the writing and journal classes, I said something about "when Terry gets out and can actually pursue a writing life."

Fay paused. I heard her take her breath in. "What?" I asked.

"Mary Anne," she approached this hard truth with the gentleness of her name (my name ironically means bittersweet), "Terry is never getting out. He's serving two life sentences."

Terry's understanding of grace suddenly fell upon my shoulders with the weight of cement. Never is such a very long time. His sense of grace and justice work like a hand sander on my own small annoyances. And I measure his never against the open slate of daily possibilities and with schooled seriousness ask myself, "What do I want to create on this day that I may long remember?" For how very true it is that most of the things which seem so significant, aren't.

Everything I needed to know in life I learned skinny dipping in the Nehalem River as a youngster. The people who loved me couldn't be seen from the river, but they were close. (Sometimes the people who love you are the same people who create conundrums in your life.) The water was always cold at first. I never eased into the cold. I always jumped in. Little bits of cold one body part at a time were excruciating; running across the dock leaping and flying for so brief a moment before torpedo–like immersing was exhilarating. (Being fully committed to any endeavor is breathtaking.) Returning to the dock against the tide always made it harder to get there. (Do the difficult thing first.)

Swimming in the Nehalem is something I always did alone. My friends would go with me in a boat or raft on the river, but not in it. It was a muddy river and very cold. And the hanging algae under the dock creeped out my girlfriends. They didn't even like bending their legs under the dock. However, I liked swimming under the dock, poking my head up between the pilings and under the planks and smelling the slippery smell and watching the way the shafts of light lit up all the life and activity in the water. (The most interesting places are the least traveled.) When I was in the river I was only thinking about being in the river. I loved the leg-paddle, standing-arm, whooshing resistance of the water against my body. (Being fully present in a moment is the finest way to enjoy it and the only way to have real fun.)

And I didn't need anything else. Even when my mischievous friend hid my clothes and throwing a fit did not get them delivered back to me, I simply stood my naked self up tall, walked up the plank, across the lawn, and into the house for other clothes. (The things that truly matter are within you, not around you. Everything is replaceable, except your breath.)

I could write that it was often lonely being in the river by myself. And that would be true. I was only lonely for awhile until I let the river be my company. If it is so, that rivers are metaphors for life, sometimes it still takes awhile for the river to remind me that I am not alone.

chances are . . . forever is . . . sitting outside my door. why am i doing the dishes? days speedily tick past. my future, ink, pours from this pen of today, written with apparent ease. a precious vapor disappears. in the clearing of it i shall see that i am aged. i shall wonder how i could have dedicated so many days to the pursuit of nonessential things. what of all those days can i recall? as i learn to embrace the gray and the wrinkle, i open the door to chance. i whisper to forever, "let's now go dance and leave the dishes for later."

Act as if someone else might have valuable insight on a view that you are certain about.

Remember the story about the four people in a small room with an elephant. Each person is certain of what they see, but they all seem to see something different. (Or, as my friend Len suggests, ask the elephant. Len reminds me that she's the one with the good memory.) Gather information for the sake of true discovery rather than to validate your tightly held opinions.

The first time I "learned" this lesson I was fairly young. Mid-twenties. Living at the coast. Caring for my ailing father and working a minimum-wage job. An artisan worked her weaving craft in a shop next to my workplace. I fell for a beautiful wrap. It was so much more than a scarf but not quite a sari. I placed a meager down payment on the piece and each pay day made an effort to free it from its space and let it wrap about my shoulders.

One rainy gray spring day, it happened. The piece was redeemed and walked out the weaver's door over my exuberant shoulders. Rich and haughty shades of blue—the color of the mountain just before dusk, the color of water at its deepest point in the spring, the richest blue of the veins of Cambozola, the kind of blue that blue becomes just before it becomes aged. This was the blue wrapped about me as I merrily strode down the small town main street. The streets were relatively empty so while I was indeed showing off—the point I was missing was that there was no one to see my show. Ah! But I heard a car coming along. There I was, waiting to be seen by . . .

Schmplat. Frumph. The cold muddied water splashed upon me like snowballs striking unexpectedly from the side while you're enjoying a winter walk. The dirty drip penetrated my mountain blue weaving to my clothes and the immediate chill added to the injury of event.

The car, not even slowing as penance for its offense, motored along main street.

"How *could* you?" My question trailed off lost in a mixture of anger and frustration.

Brand new. Six months' worth of patient payments and . . . I looked down into the street from the very edge of the sidewalk where I had been prancing along in the light spring rain. Earlier that day a Pacific Northwest deluge had occurred and the streets were deeply puddled and potholed with sand, mud runoff from the creek, and all other street-appropriate rubble.

In that instant, which came flashingly and convincingly from lifelong learning, I knew my anger was born of taking something personally that was not personal at all. While I was undeniably personally wet, it was a simple confluence of events, which singularly had nothing to do with me or the car, but rather with the impersonal alchemy of the two combining in a single moment.

Here's the trick: applying that lesson to this. Having the clarity at the edge of the pointed comment to recognize the hurt is not about me as much as it is about the person speaking the hurt. Even in instances when the sounds of the words or the direction of the action seems ultimately personal—it's not. This knowledge has allowed me the presence of mind to walk away, unscathed, from many potentially explosive situations.

I loved. For this presence whom I loved I wrote, "When I say I am going home, what I mean is I am going to where you are." How well I meant that. There was a time when that was true about the individual. But then it wasn't. Spectrum shot of hurt. I tried to grasp that his decisions were not personal, intending harm for me. They were an expression of wounds and needs and lessons in his life. While they significantly impacted me, they were not for me. They were mud splattered upon the weaving, the precious, blue-mountain, newly redeemed weaving, I was wrapped in. Mud splattered while motoring or perhaps speeding on the way to somewhere else. Some other home that was not me or my or our home. Ultimately, this shook me. And after my questions and questionings, angers and frustrations were yelled at the back of the speeding car. I turned to the *R* in my planning book and read again and again . . .

"Don't take it personally—it's not usually about you."

The key word is "usually." Sometimes it is personal. Sometimes it is about you. That's the real conundrum of the lesson—knowing when it is and when it isn't. That "knowing" comes to each person wrapped a different way.

My friend, Jonathan Huie, expresses the sense of "don't take it personally" in his poem.

The River of Life (excerpted)
The River of Life flows without emotion.
The River surges. The River quiets.
The River overflows its banks. The River dries to a trickle.
The River swirls and storms. The River becomes calm.
The River runs clear. The River runs dark.
The River is indifferent to what benefit or what harm is
    caused by its water.
The River is the River, and that is all there is to it.

The River of Life knows no obstacles.
The River can cut through solid rock—in its own time.

The River of Life is not powerful—and it is not weak.
The River of Life is not gentle—and it is not strong or rough.
The River of Life is not deep or shallow.
The River of Life is not nourishing or punishing.
The River of Life is simply the River of Life.
The River of Life just IS. There is no more to it.

One can flow harmoniously with the River—or one can
struggle fearfully against the River—and the River just
flows.
One can accept the River—or one can deny the River—and
the River just flows.
One can worship the River of Life—or one can curse the
River of Life—and the River just flows.
I choose to flow with the River of Life.

—Jonathan Huie (2003—inspired by
Byron Katie's School for the Work)

List the things that seem overwhelming to you on this day.
Look at it again in a month. Consider your view toward those
items in that time.

Defer gratification on something. Find out if you want it
as much in six weeks as you do today. Actively work on your
perspective by asking yourself, "How significant will this thing
be in five years, one year, next month?"

pay attention

the pleiades
perhaps this is how we
lose our way in the world—
    it is unremembered
    since I have seen the
    milky way.

time ago
i walked out my home
into the night and
kept company with
the pleiades.

i am not now certain
where i might look for
that once familiar constellation.

we lose our way
in the world slowly—
    insidiously.
it comes upon a soul like
a bulb planted last winter—
while busy growing it is unnoticed
and suddenly there's a riot of color
where once was a blanket of snow.
    forgetting is like that.
    it happens soporifically.
    and then you are startled—

awakened to what you
once possessed and
now, no longer have:
a riot of absence.

some of the stars are obscured by urbanity—
civilized light snuffs the milky way.

others are there, still, but a form of
dementia takes my eyes.

pleiades, sisters, am i looking right at you
and unknowing of your forms?

pleiades, are you there?
is that you?
is it?
speak to me, yes, one of you just whisper,
"i am here. we are . . . we are here."
following your voice perhaps
i can trace your forms
with my fingers.

yes, dear seven sisters, in your
brilliant company,
it comes back to me.

in this sparkling remembering
presses a sense of
  where to find
  the milky way.

    i must begin looking
    in the dark—
    in the wilded, uncitied dark.

———————

with passion live
with attentiveness love
with courage imagine
with integrity communicate
with perspective play
in all things and in all your ways
build your legacy with joy.

———————

this day with my words . . .
when you speak—tell the story of your life.
when you communicate—speak the truth.
unite not divide.
be certain of information.
utilize discernment, not judgment.
speak for those who cannot speak on their own behalf.
write to learn your truth.
and when you speak, speak with truth.
bring no harm.

With so many words, it is easy to come to them casually. Lorrena Thompson, a body worker who helps people claim their own path to growth, has a powerful statement about the impact, the currency, of our words. She says:

> *There are so many words in the universe and they each hold a space and call their likeness to them. If I am going to add to this collection, then may it call in love, may it attract wholeness.*

If I had a friend named Attentive, I would describe him thus: Attentive listens pointedly. To any matter at hand he says, "You are the only matter to which I will pay heed. I will hear you."

Other plans and just-sparked memories and things he is just about ready to say do not weave in and out of Attentive's mind. Careful attention is paid. There are interruptions made only if clarification is required. Sometimes, at the end of the day, Attentive is particularly tired. Listening and comprehending take a great deal of skill and energy. However, it could be no other way. Attentive says, "I believe anything to which I choose to pay attention deserves my full self. I will invest nothing less."

Remember people's names. Correctly. In remembering you demonstrate an unusual type of respect and show value for individuality. Particularly remember the name of a child. In this you are teaching a child of their significance. A name is a basic validation. Don't presume to change someone's name. If you are introduced to Kenneth, do not call him Ken.

Say thank you when you are complimented. Do not disagree or correct. Respect the opinion that has been expressed by responding graciously.

i lean forward
full of the
possibility, the
hope of color,
growth, warmed soil
and being loose of
the chill of this
garden's long winter.

i have chosen many of the dark, difficult places in which I have
stood. And while I have emerged from those dark places,
owning the willingness to stand there is very significant to
understanding the whole of the things to be learned. No one teth-
ered me in those places against my will. Growth and maturity
exist largely in knowing when it is time to walk. Knowing when
to leave. There is a peculiar grace in knowing when it is time to say
good-bye to a thing, a person, a system, a construct, a belief.

I often hear people speak of relationships at their conclusion as
"failed." Simply because a thing does not last until its anticipated
conclusion, that does not make it a failure. If a flower is crushed
while still in bloom, it is not a failed flower. When a younger life
is slashed off the planet by a knife or bullet, it doesn't mean that
that life failed in its presence on the planet. It is indeed a loss to
those who remain, but it is not failure. A relationship must be
allowed its cycle and time. Not all comings together are forever
even though we bind them to that in our societal vocabulary. The
human being whose life is now lived far from my life and whose
name is not a part of my name has his own story. And his parting
was less a failure than a learning.

Friendships are a vehicle. They travel you to places you never imagined . . . both in the literal and figurative sense. And friends are the road or path itself. It can be a path that circles the globe or one that ends in a beautiful pass in the Ohio Valley. It's easier to see when looking back.

There are some friends in our lives without whom we cannot imagine our days; and then our days take care of the "without them" all on their own. Moving, differing relationships, illness, death . . . there are so many conditions that can tear apart what seemed seamless.

I remember one such friendship that felt seamless but eventually was gently torn.

We were each eating a Sunday morning cookie and reading the newspaper. Somewhere a few pages in, not on the front page, in just a few column inches, was the announcement that the Federal Government planned to issue leases off the coasts of Oregon and Washington. What? We read again what little information was there just to be certain we had understood the undesirable implications.

"We're going to be another Santa Barbara? This is terrible." Carol Ann assessed.

This was impacting news to both of us. We were each water babies. We chose to live in a small community by the sea. Carol Ann surfed and I body boarded. We loved the sea for reasons we didn't even understand at the time.

"How can they just *do* this?" she asked.

"They can't," I replied.

"Well, they are."

"We'll stop them."

"Like we could stop them."

"Yes. We can stop them."

I didn't know how. But I knew we could. Community service had been woven into my life, but not activism. I acted *for* things, not *against* them. I didn't know anything about that. We agreed that we would meet early in the week, each armed with what information we'd been able to collect, and we would ask ourselves the weighted question, "What can we do?"

And here's what the answer to that question turned out to be:

We collected twenty-five thousand signatures opposing oil drilling off the coasts, mobilized an entire community, founded a volunteer group called the Energy Project to create alternative energy options to the oil, which *might* have been discovered off the coast, put in place a community shuttle that operated solely on natural gas, and made a trip to Washington D.C., to meet with elected officials and policy makers—and to present our stack of petitions.

We made a difference. And we created an opportunity for countless others to make a difference. The leases were deferred. And recently, when the moratorium on the leases ran out, others picked up the fight.

Two friends, having a breakfast cookie and reading a newspaper took a journey neither could have imagined. We changed our world view and each other.

In the subsequent years, our paths parted. It wasn't a fussy parting, or one that we particularly noticed over time. It was a gentle shift. And when I moved away and she moved away—it was a true parting. It's been many years since we have seen each other, but I still wear the bracelet she gifted me after we returned from

Washington D.C. and learned the news that our efforts had been successful.

State government representatives urged me to run for elected office. The leadership of various organizations solicited me for a long time to become involved in other environment causes. I declined. Their disappointment turned to criticism.

"You were so effective in this effort. How can you turn your back on these issues when they need you? We need you."

The world is full of need. And I know I must answer the calls for help that I recognize. But to simply continue in my life picking up causes like so many waiting shells and polished stones on a walk along the beach—no, I couldn't do it. The cause, the reason for the activism, had to stir something within me. And my actions had to be an answer to that stirring. Being an activist wasn't a hobby, it was an answer. I let the objections continue to be levied, and I walked away.

In that walking away from being wanted, from being "selected," from that sense of fulfilling an important destiny (even though it was someone else's sense of destiny for me), I changed. I learned.

Poet Karah G. Fisher expresses this process so well in the following poem.

Like this beach
Smoothed sparse by winter storms,
I have emerged more naked to the world—
Cloaks of clutched identities
now dropped from my shoulders.
Pockets emptied of ideological baubles,
once hoarded against the insecurities

of unknowns and voicelessness.
Loved ones step cautiously, fingering
my clutter of dropped doctrinal hoardings
and long-worn substitutes for selfhood.
Like me, they didn't ask for this new task—
to make sense of my surprise discarding,
to try and trust this new bare truth.
Some don't have time for grief, or room.
I understand.
We hold what we can.
The rest we let go.

It was time for me to leave. And what I was leaving was so delicious in its appearance. The opportunity to be a part-time hero is reasonably appealing. I chose to be hero to myself. I chose to not disappoint myself. And in so choosing, disappointed others. Such is just one consequence of knowing when to leave.

Learning her own version of this lesson, this knowing when to leave, in spring of 2006, Gina writes via email from Darfur:

My days have been busier than at any other point in my life, and I feel it. It's been a great challenge for me, in many ways, to have Diego gone for twenty days. Managing the workload and the budget/donor issues with London and the UN coordination issues alone would have been a tall order. Then last Thursday (the 13th) the Chadian rebels decided to attack Chad in an attempt to overthrow the government. The fighting along the border was heavy, and we were close to evacuation. Really close. So, we had a few days fully consumed by that.

And now we're kind of waiting, the dress rehearsal already under our belts, for another attempt.

At noon, our local staffer, Abdulrahim, is still with us. The BBC is announcing that the rebels have reached the parliament building in N'djamena, the capital of Chad. We've prepared everything for evacuation, but the mortars have stopped. The four "relocatable" staff, two drivers and two guards are cooking themselves a chicken.

I go to speak with Abdulrahim, who is smoking another cigarette under the shade, reading the copy of Kapuscinski's *Shadow of the Sun*. I handed it to him two hours ago, when I knew we were in for long hours of waiting. He has his Motorola handset hooked to his belt, his delicate glasses tucked into his shirt pocket, and his feet up on the table. I tell him that the BBC is reporting the fall of N'Djamena. I'm stupidly and momentarily jubilant because at least a rebel victory would mean calm on the border and the end to our evacuation plans. But Abdulrahim's hand is trembling. Because this is what it would really mean: A killing field in the camps of eastern Chad, Janjaweed control of the entire territory, the end to any hope for the Darfuri rebels, the beginning of more loss for thousands.

There's so much I don't understand here, so much I don't fully see. Rebels had been gathering for this attack for weeks. We all knew that their numbers were increasing . . .

So much dangerous politics.

On Thursday afternoon, while the rest of us remain in lock-down, Abdulrahim prepares to make his way home to his family. I stop him to shake his hand and he makes the effort of a weak smile. He's the only one that hasn't taken the events of today lightly.

The next day, when the world has turned calm again (for the moment), he passes by to visit after his Friday prayers. And as if nothing at all had happened, as if we hadn't turned him away, he flashes a sly, conspiratorial smile, and whispers, "The rebels were defeated. This is good news."

I met privately with Abdulrahim today. Rebels are regrouping in West Darfur and are preparing for another offensive. The borders will be the first, hard fight.

But we've already rehearsed the tough part, myself and Abdulrahim. Now at least we know what to expect of each other. He knows that if the real war starts, I'll take my free ticket of escape. I know that he'll hide his disappointment and forgive me one day.

It is a peculiar wisdom that alerts us to that moment in time. That moment when we know it is time for us to leave.

Practice appropriate departure. Learn to see your own signs and know how to set a thing down. Change your patterns. If you don't like gossip, practice leaving when it starts. Make a decision to leave based upon your understanding of your purpose, not upon the perception of others of your departure. Take note of how you feel as you leave. And after you have gone.

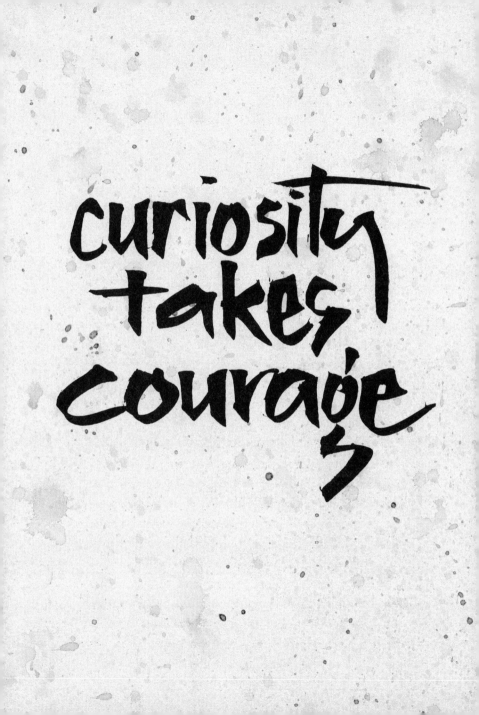

you lean forward not because you know, but because you
    want to find out.
you lean forward into your life not because it is safe to do so,
    but because
you have found it intolerable to remain still, unmoving from
    the same place.

(remember when the spacecraft fell from the sky to texas?)
    i weep that we americans seem to be defined more by
what we have collectively lost than by what we hold as a
whole. how is it that we can call ourselves champions? on
this day i weep for our american star which fell from the
texas sky. (they say everything is bigger there. i wonder if
their grief is larger than mine?) i remember this loss from
my childhood. i remember the fear of throwing lives into
the sky and wondering if they could possibly find their
way home. how these decades of progress have jaded my
wonderment, my sense of risk.
    perhaps my loss impairs my vision. there is a spark
of hopefulness in this tragedy. it is the true spirit of a
champion which allows us to continue to explore. after
such collective loss we still wish to be pathfinders. we still
long to answer questions and blaze a new way of seeing. we
still reach nonpartisan hands across borders and invite, "let
us be bigger together than we are alone."
    we are victors in this: that tomorrow we will reach
again for the stars and be sobered by this loss to reach for
a higher excellence—ask bigger questions and work, like
champions, for the discovery of the answer.

where will i find the goodness? i must sing in my own soul. the vastness, the breadth to match the demands of my days. that, too, must rise from within me. strength and courage are gifts. they are gifts that can be enhanced by a friend. at their core they must come from within me.

rumi said, "let the beauty you love be what you do."

that is the reason we are on this earth.

the breath you breathe in this moment is why we are on this earth. and the shoulder you touch . . . that community.

the drop of blood which drips when you are pricked . . . that pain.

the laughter that spontaneously erupts from an unexpected joy . . . those joys.

you can be so busy hunting for volcanoes that you do not see the fire in front of you. live a life of passion—explore it by setting aside rigidity and analysis. it will never make sense in the moment and it might not make sense when it's all done. only in the loving action is there reason.

Ask. Inquire. Take the opportunity to expand your knowledge by digging a little deeper. Look at your days as an equation and start wondering what would happen if you changed some of the components. (The phrase, "do the math," can take on a whole new meaning.) If you find yourself saying, "I've always wondered why . . ." Research. Discover. Answer your own questions.

the most
important
promises
are the ones
you make to
yourself

i will sing.
i will dance.
i will laugh.
i will laugh again.
i will give and receive with grace.
i will learn and fail with enthusiasm.
i will converse and reflect equally.
i will move with grace and strength.
i will sit with ease and purpose.
i will give without obligation and will
    receive without encumbrance.
i will imagine and believe.
i will listen and embrace.
i will heal and be healed.
i will live the contradictions while understanding
    it is all the same thing.

—————

somebody lied to you once.
once. but it was a really really big lie.
you know it. you know the one of which i speak.
it's the one that began,
    "that's not good enough."
and the great brown sadness is that
you believed that lie.
and now you are just finishing up the days trying
to be good enough. the glory of the inside of a
murex has invited you to your own glory.
the shell's inner soul reminds you of what you have always

known but weren't brave enough to believe . . .
you are perfect just as you are.
you are a glorious,
        creative, dancing, laughing being . . .
who loves chocolate and children and animals and
friends and frosts all those cakes with loving frosting
for others but forgets to keep a slice for herself.
look in that precious mirror and say
when i first saw you i knew you'd arrive today . . .
just fine.
just perfect.
the way you are.
remember this day
is your wild and precious gift.
open it and honor it.
remember this day
is your opportunity to
grow and learn and be better
at dusk than you were at dawn.
remember this day
that to extending
important as receiving love.

———————

i am willing.
    i am willing to craft a body which can leap and hike
and kayak and be strong and resilient.
    i am willing to practice my natural gifts without
reservation. i am willing to love with courage and
compassion and set aside pettiness and judgment. i am

willing to be incorrect for the sake of discovery; i am
willing to fail for the emergence of innovation. i am
willing to balance contradiction in order to experience
success, prosperity, equanimity, satisfying exchanges
between true hearts.

    i will sing.

———————

remember this day
there isn't a soul
on the earth that smiles or
laughs the way you do.

remember this day
that you are the creator
and the joys will hold
the memories that will
be written with your pen.
the pen of this day.

cherish the endings knowing they are
always followed by beginnings.

keep company with and deepen your listening for
those creatures whose presence brings beauty to the land.

breathe in the winds of courage
that each day you may discover
in fresh ways what it is to
soar above this sacred earth
and sweetly land in her
arms at dusk.

to acknowledge all living things
    and be kind.

to tell the truth of the seasons
    with the work of my hands

to tell forth the celebration of the earth
    with the movement of my body

to tell my mind to become lost
    so that i may enter into that
        sacred space of creating.

Operate from plenty today, extend your finest gifts, best attentiveness, and hard listening. Look at the events of your day and see them for their instruction. Speak less and listen more. Eat less and be nurtured more. Hear more of the goodness, which the earth sings out. Hear the cries of the oppressed and have a hand to reach them or a voice to speak for them. Speak no harm. Inspire and be inspired. Challenge the edges of your comfort. Choose your roles rather than having them assigned. Celebrate the day and the holy opportunity of each moment. Be lover and loved, teacher and student, magician and apprentice. Take away the breath of those you touch and fill their lungs with ocean spray. Have and be a following sea.

appreciation
lasts
longer than
complaint

there is nothing as respectful as the sound of a door shutting softly.

let me pause just long enough to notice the sweet small thing which you have done well and right. and then let me notice it to you.

*a*uthor James Crumley asserts that you only need nine friends—one to count cadence and eight to carry the coffin. Look around you. Who would your nine be? And the opinions of those beyond that truly do not matter. (Pay no heed to the opinions of others.) That small circle of nine is the circle which merits, in fact, requires my appreciation to grow. And it is their appreciation which, in turn, comes to mean so much to my personal development.

Be specifically grateful. Express gratitude to yourself and to those around you. Gratitude and appreciation are the lights in the dark corners in each day. Close out each day adding to a list of things for which you are specifically grateful. Try experiencing gratitude toward difficulty. Be thankful for the opportunity to learn, to grow. Practice saying to absolute strangers who have done something well, "I appreciate that."

What are you willing to lose in order to taste your own realization? You know the name of your dream. At what cost will you speak that name loudly?

It comes down to security as compared to satisfaction. What is known versus what is possible. Dependable versus unpredictable. What will you set aside in order to embrace the potential of your passion? It comes without a guarantee: is that why it is considered risk?

You have to open your hand, dropping your tightly held assumptions, expectations, aspirations, and grasped certainty in order to free your palm to host the butterfly. If your fist is closed, the promises fly by—unable to land.

What will you set down in order to host hope?

I am willing to be isolated. I am willing to sully my reputation. I am willing to provide no defense or explanation addressing the expectations of others. I am willing to be misunderstood, not chosen, even set aside. I willingly exchange these things for the yes I extend to myself. The resolute yes of answering the longing of my heart, being able to be cast out from convention in order that I not be cast out from my own spirit.

I am willing to answer the incredulous question, "How could you . . . ?" with the even more incredulous response, "How could I not?"

> if it is this day alone of which I have a certainty
>
> then it is a greater risk to not act from personal courage.
>
> greater than the burden of a failed dream is the burden of regret
>
> over a dream not attempted.

What am I willing to lose in order to taste my own realization? Because I am not afraid to die my answer must be, "I am willing to lose everything." And said in another way the answer is also, "I am willing to gain everything."

In either instance I guess that's why it is called risk.

Recognize that acting according to your purpose sometimes means acting out of sync with others. Unclench your teeth and simply say what is on your mind. Be aware of civility and connect to your truth. If something is not acceptable simply say, "This is not acceptable."

Understand the difference between tolerance and allowing mediocrity a plot in your garden.

Surprise is as powerful as consistency

there is no small kindness. a compassionate act makes large
the world.

The days march into spring. There are moments, especially early in the morning, when Winter seems reluctant to release its tenacious hold on his younger sister, Spring. "Who knows what kind of mischief she might get into if I really let her loose," Winter wonders.

Fond of her, yet not understanding her ways, he likes the comfort and certainty of the grays and white of snow and the silver of sideways rain. Spring goes about, indiscriminately it appears, splashing color. This way and that. And all that awakening! Of hope, passion, activity.

Who knew the surprise of jumping up and down on a sofa would create such a stir? In a culture/society where it's "cool" to appear cool . . . distant . . . disassociated, the unabashed enthusiasm that Tom Cruise demonstrated in his jumping up and down created levels of discomfort. The global audience, while drawn to the sensational, is more comfortable with the consistent. The enthusiasm displayed by Mr. Cruise, without embarrassment or apology, made others embarrassed. I loved it. I still get a kick out of it, after much time has passed, hearing people bring it up. I admire him, an individual subjected to extraordinary scrutiny, willing to shine forth genuinely instead of simply meeting expectation. In Tom Cruise's case surprise turned out to be more powerful than consistency.

It took me a period of six months to create the distinctive lettering style, which has come to be associated with my original writings. In the nine years I'd been in business I had been very protective about teaching the form to anyone else. I was proprietary.

Events conspired to hand me a remarkable, unprecedented episode of arthritis. It became increasingly debilitating. I was performing the role of Anna in a community production of *The King and I*. The polka was a peculiar challenge in an iron skirt and layers of period costume, representing pounds on my frame.

As I neared the end of rehearsing the theater production, which I was committed to completing, it was becoming difficult to even hold a pen. Having this commitment to not teach anyone to write my stylized lettering had become a conundrum.

One sunny spring day a young lady entered my public studio. I thought she was eleven. I learned soon enough that she was seventeen and was about to graduate from high school. Timidly she offered a confession. She was a peer counselor in her high school and as a freshman started using my writings in her volunteer work. As a sophomore she began to copy my lettering and over the years, mastered my lettering style. She assured me she had never used it commercially, only in her volunteer work. It took some time for her to come to the real point of the confession.

She was hoping to come work for me for the summer before she entered college. What a surprise! I had doggedly kept to my standard of keeping my lettering to myself and when I needed it most, here was a delightful soul whose writing looked every bit like mine. I had her letter some things and could barely tell the difference between her hand and mine. That young lady was Gina Bramucci. Gina, the young lady who came to work for me when she was seventeen.

Gina's presence in my life and company that summer allowed my hands and body the time that was needed to kick that malady out of my bones. She's been a uniquely healing presence in my life from then to now.

Surprize (yes, with a z) does things differently on purpose.
Remember the view from inside a rut is boring. New vistas are important. Read about new locations and scientific discoveries. Read about things with which you are not familiar. Act as if you are adept at solving problems. See an old thing in a new way.

listen
to your
inclination

we are remembered from the ways we have walked our ideals.

at the heart of history is this reminder—you paint the colors of
your days.

recognize that your spiritual self is a crucial voice in the whole
of your life. Recognize what you believe and begin to com-
prehend why you believe it. Your spirituality is intrinsic to growth,
the process of change, creative expression—all essential processes
of living.

from perspective comes unusual courage.
from a place of isolation
comes unexpected breathless beauty.
for all the times you have sewn strings on the buttons of
my spirit . . .
for all the roots you have nurtured,
for all the ways you helped me to see dirt
as an opportunity to grow.
you teach so many ways of thinking
paths to learning.
having you as a teacher has given me
the vision and the strength to teach . . . and
the courage to learn.

———————

there is synthesis.
there is silence.
then there are spaces
in between the two.

those spaces require the greatest courage.
for in them we
must learn to listen
to ourselves.

we write the tales of our lives with our daily activities.
we speak deeply of our lives through the stories we tell.

I have named God many different ways in my life. This diverse naming provides me a fundamental hopefulness. In the utter encompassing place in which God dwells—I am grateful for the confidence that this very godness allows him to know his name when it is called.

As a true heart calls out the name of God, God hears—regardless of the consonants, regardless of the language, when it is spoken earnestly. In this hearing, we must trust the godness of God.

How is it I know God?

I know God because at a moment in time I turned my head to God at the precise moment his head was inclined toward me.

Some disciplines call that being born again. I call it coming home. On a particular day in my history I came to an intimacy with God. And the closer I have come to knowing him, the less I am compelled to speak of it.

As my eyesight has broadened and the roots of my belief have grown about my spirit—I prefer the silence and a solitary sanctuary.

How is it that one is able to articulate the landscape of the spirit? The geography of the heart is understood and seen in ways which are, essentially, ineffable. Such understanding is a journey, a discovery, a joy: peculiar and particular. In our spirits' holy night

sky we come to know the singular beauty and magic that is our
own music.

life is sacred: live on purpose. be intoxicated with this
world and astonished with the world you imagine. growth
is a journey . . . success doesn't require arrival. want what
you already hold. give no place to public opinion. delight
in your friends. practice the art of doing nothing. embrace
moments of grace. give the child in you a wide sky.
understand that laughter is prayer.
—*co-authored with Terry Hershey*

I am certain that Annie Dillard in *The Writing Life* was quoting
some ancient wisdom, a knowing so old that it is unattributable in
its source, when she explained, "How you spend this hour is how
you spend your life."

Kris King of Eugene, Oregon-based Wings Seminars explains
it this way: "How you do anything is how you do everything." I've
cryptically told myself, without even being sure what it meant,
"Everything about this is everything about that." And that bourbon-
swilling, cigar-puffing consultant I worked with as a twenty-
something often touted, "Settle for disorder in lesser things for the
sake of order in greater things."

Just from these words I draw some instruction of the process
of right practice. One person's wisdom and master, so suited for
them, is not the fit master for someone else. A master who teaches
well at one point on a life journey may not be the apt teacher for
another point. And the right way, which is true and good on Sunday may not be the best choice on Tuesday.

To wander without rigidity and have the courage to discover the master's wisdom in the day is my right practice. Those whose ways are different consider this path folly, or heresy or, at least, inconsistent. Some find in the variable nature of my walking something they are willing to call lack of discipline, or lack of true faith, or some such assessment. Others turn their eye to my way and call me a visionary, a mystic, or one who sees with a different heart. There is a lesson I can draw from these assessments. One must not be defined, determined, or deterred by the views and opinions of others. It is great work to come to know one's own heart, how can another truly know it? It is the broad and true glimpses into the real heart of another, which create ribbons of intimacy and tie us, gently. And in those ties we come to know clear and certain truth. There's right practice in that. Right practice is not a rigid set of ethics that one applies, like poured concrete, to a path. But rather it is the light that shines upon any chosen path. And like the sun, at different seasons and in progressive times in the day, its light shines from a different place. Regardless of the angle of its shine, it is light. Standing in that light is my right practice.

Recognize that habit inhibits your ability to see your beliefs clearly. Pay attention. Take the time to be clear on your beliefs—do not act from assumption or pattern. Listen to your inclination (or whatever you call it) (what do you call it?). Determine a short period of time that you will listen intensely to your quiet sense of things. Take note of how many times you can act upon it and what the consequences appear to be. Be a mirror for others and experiment with inviting their own quiet inclination.

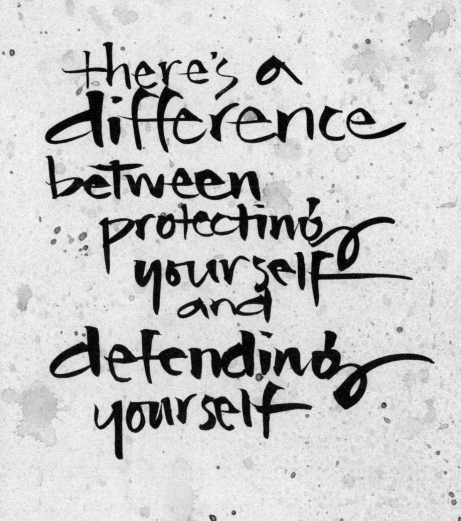

there's a
difference
between
protecting
yourself
and
defending
yourself

the patterns are most of my own choosing,
the weave is complex and extraordinary,
the elegance is defined by my own sense of style,
the vision is far reaching and deeply impacting,
i meet the paradox of my moments with strength,
    compassion, and courage.

I n a period of time when my best efforts were met by a small
group with a large voice of disapproval, I offered one attempt
at defense. In that effort, I was not allowed the opportunity
to speak. In that moment, I purposed I would offer no further
defense, ever, since the offer of my voice was refused.

In a greater context, it's a privilege to be philosophically or
structurally attacked. (I am not speaking of a physical attack, but
a cultural or societal or political one.) It speaks to the fact that
something about me is different. Something about me requires
people to offer some explanation for their view of me. I'm not an
order-marching member of a pack. I am my father's daughter. He
learned the real difference between being respectful in a civil sense
and extending one's respect because an individual has earned it.

From whom have I taken my greatest lesson? Whose respect,
affection, and esteem mean the most to me? Whose advice do I
seek? The answers to these questions comprise the circle of people
whose opinions matter to me. Those beyond that circle are only
significant in the power they hold to impact my vision and goals.
Beyond this small circle I have come to a place where I offer no
defense.

In my commitment to my own vision I must accept that the
commitments of others will certainly not always be in accord with

my own. I can only tell my own story. And I can only grow in the soil of my own knowing. It is here where I must echo the words I co-authored with Terry Hershey: "Give no heed to the opinions of others." This is not an endorsement to not learn from others. It is a reminder that there will always be naysayers who travel opposing roads simply in principle. Or those whose roads dramatically differ from mine. I remind myself those roads are their stories. I choose my own road. And for this, there is no defense.

Here follows a correspondence of letters, penned in a mailed journal called Circle Journey, between me and my dear friend Gina who over this time of writing went from home in Oregon, to school in Missouri, to work as a journalist in an aid organization in Uganda, then into humanitarian aide herself. The correspondence begins with a quote from an artist that Gina didn't know that I had met! In this correspondence Gina and I struggle to explore the balance between protecting oneself and reaching for one's vision. And our exploration moves from the discourse of the small life experience to the large issue of protection and defense embodied in our own patriotism, which we labored to understand in light of attack and war.

Gina places this quote in the beginning of the small mailable book:

> *Which is more artistic: to make an imaginative work of art or to live an imaginative life?*
>
> *—Kazuaki Tanahashi*

Five years ago I may have thought of me, now, as cynical. My cynicism has become my enlightenment. The more hope I lose the more hopeful I become. An irony I understand better in the living than the telling. By savoring my solitude more—I

become better with people. Contrasts and contradictions make
greater sense to me. I am still shocked by certain betrayals, but
I more expect most people to have a knife somewhere and, at
some time, answer to the endearment, "You too, Brutus?"

Expect disloyalty, Gina, and you will be blessed with those
who are true. To know that there is darkness in every heart lets
you more clearly see the light in every heart.

Good bye, God, Gina has gone to Missouri.

Gina writes back on August 28, 2001.

. . . and to know that there is hidden good in the world IS
light. "Infinite goodness has such wide arms."

                                                    —Dante
To know the dark is, I think, simply to be honest and real.
But it seems to me that the more difficult task is to discover
light even in the darkest shadows. Maybe that is essentially
what you're saying. Still, I don't want to—I can't—expect
disloyalty from people. By expecting the most someone has to
offer, I open the door for that hidden goodness. If I anticipated
that ugly face of disloyalty, betrayals, hurt, I would invite
them in. So often people will give what they sense is expected
or predicted. I might sound incredibly naive and idealistic,
but I hope I don't lose these ideals. The most astonishing
thing in Africa was that these people—people who have lost
children, parents, siblings, spouses, and friends at the hands of
rebels or AIDS—continue to laugh, to sing, and to hope for
peace. They weep, they pray, they continue. If I take one lesson
from them, I would like it to be the ability to see light.

And so "my train" rolls forward (off the track or on it) to
that person I become that you mention so often. Right now
I'm wearing a t-shirt that I've owned all the years I've known
you. It's seen as much as you, and I wonder what that picture
looks like from a distance. If there's one thing to be said for us
both—ours have not been predictable journeys. I never would
have (could have) imagined where we would be today if you
had asked me that night on the train.

   Life can be a little like that travel game we used to play
flipping through Condé Nast and your travel journals. Pick a
destination and for five full minutes, maybe ten, it's yours. I'm
trying more and more, though, to accept that no matter how
hard I try, I'll never read a map exactly right. But didn't we
stumble on the best parts of Italy by getting lost?

I wrote her back on September 7.

   It's too easy to carry out the obvious metaphor that one
stumbles into the better parts of their lives by being lost.
(Didn't someone "famous" say in being lost I am found?)
So often we don't know we are looking for a thing until
we accidentally happen upon it. Then it's some universal
recognition, the ohmygod I've been longing for this my whole
life!!! And I didn't know the recognition, the thisness, of it
until I saw it.

   As to these gloves of apparent cynicism I wear, let me say
this—you speak in karmic terms of you get what you expect.
So let me restate. Be anticipatory of betrayal. Be aware. Be
conscious. Have the understanding that the stranger with

whom you speak is neither wholly dark nor wholly light.
While I am more cynical now than I have ever been I am also
happier. Less and less do I deal in disappointment in others. I
am more realistically anticipatory of their behavior. Less often
I am inclined to be shocked, taken aback. Conversely I am
more often met with surprise or delight than my expectation.
My anticipation has been far exceeded. Brother Lawrence,
a 15th-century monk, said that rather than being surprised
that people kill each other, we should instead be surprised
that more people don't kill each other more often. Our history,
of the whole world, is one of self-interest, betrayals, and
articulated darkness. It is bliss to see light, hope, promise in
such darkness. And the light certainly exists. It is quixotic to
expect there to always be light hidden in the darkness. Therein
lies the difference in our views.

In another vernacular I am suggesting you take the stance
of a martial artist. At ready. Balanced. Focused. Not poised to
attack but, there's the word . . . anticipatory. If your hands are
held correctly you are always ready—ready to deflect a knife
and ready to open a gift. Perhaps I should instead call my
brand of cynicism "readiness."

Here it is, another morning and I'm still ready to consider
this contrast of dark and light. Exploring the expectation of
good versus the anticipation betrayal. Let me suggest that by
the word betrayal I mean any intent toward you that is not
in your best interest, that is not "good." It's not my wish to
perpetuate the pessimism that permeates the world.

A teacher does not stand before a new class and expect
everyone to perform in the upper 2 percent. A true soul

cannot, should not, stand before the world and expect utter goodness. It defies the odds. There is a natural balance. There is light in the dark places. Conversely there is dark within the light. Walking into a dark room is never a challenge if one has a candle, a flashlight. What I am suggesting is a tool of an attitude to enable you to walk safely in the world.

Can we compromise and agree to believe in hope, and believe in the finest from others while also being prepared for their less than best . . . or worst? For preparation is not equal to expectation, is it? And it is a broad-spectrum view that allows you to be anticipatory of many outcomes, not simply a single possibility.

Now, as to my expectation for myself . . . there is another matter. For there I always expect my own best. And most certainly I know the taste of disappointment when it is not the best I deliver up.

How is it that we walk our days seeking that which substantiates our already held beliefs rather than courageously challenging our assumptions and seeking views through new lenses. "Ahhha, I thought so!" "Yes, that's what I thought all along."

I think of Rabbit from A. A. Milne's Winnie the Pooh tales. Rabbit, who is always right and for whom all information, no matter how contradictory, supports his views. Absolutism breeds prejudice because it asserts in action and assumes in philosophy that only one view can be correct. There is no place for dichotomy. For how can two opposing views be correct. And of course there in only one truth (as long as it is my truth). Acknowledgment of the legitimacy of many ways

would lead to (gasp) tolerance. And what would become of
America then? For myself, I vacillate between walking many
different paths without seeking defense or asserting judgment
and seeing that I am highly judgmental, almost snobbish, at
many counts, in regard to ethical views and myopic moral
positions. So I too sit in a chair validating my own variety
of beliefs. An ancient Middle Eastern phrase, "Life is life,"
comes to mind. It is just what it is. Such is a goal of Taoist
principle . . . to operate naturally, with understanding and no
understanding, of the "way of things." Have you noticed there
aren't so many saints being recognized in these days?

On December 7, Gina wonders in pen from school:
I think we're all craving the comfort of what we know. (It's
not that I sit and think constantly about this. I just think it's
an interesting impact that, hopefully, is challenging people to
stretch their thinking a bit. It's funny too . . . my world was
infinitely less secure in Uganda, but I expected that and was
constantly aware of it. Somehow it's different when it begins to
touch once-sacred parts of our lives.)

I wrote to Gina on February 8, 2002.
Had a wordshop tonight—Journaling for the Writing
Reluctant. It was comprised of eight rather earnest
writers—nearly all of whom had one or more unfinished
novels. Learning this, I told them the second half of the class
was tomorrow morning at seven. We'd be meeting to walk
the eighteen miles to Silverton—and then back. By noon.
Ludicrous? Of course. We'd need fitness training. Many

smaller walks to work up to such a large walk. Could we do
it? Yes, we could do it. Could we do it tomorrow? Not likely.
"How is it we come to have such unreasonable and unfounded
expectations for ourselves?" I asked. "What is it about writing
a novel that makes us think we can simply start out with that?
Start out with Everest instead of a training hill?" They got it.

On May 21, Gina wrote:

I've been reading Elie Wiesel. He writes:

"And yet. My two favorite words applicable to every
situation." So much of his writing points out this truth. The
"and yet" of life. In his assertion that the sun rises, he notes
with his "and yet," that it will also set. In the balance of all
contradictory things he believes, "the important thing is to
shun resignation, to refuse to wallow in sterile fatalism." I
can't help but wonder—do all rivers run to the sea?

On June 9, I wrote to Gina.

I wrote a much older friend and asked her candid advice. I've
become so frustrated at apparently repeating my mistakes. I
thought you would enjoy what she had to say to me.

As I look upon you it is almost as if I have become an
unconventional English woman and I see you as a brash
American woman. So impatient. I know you don't see
yourself as impatient and that's actually one of your
troubles. The depth of your impatience reaches to the
questions you ask of me. "When am I going to learn?" The
answer is a contradiction. Always. Never. If your life song
wasn't the same song, umpteenth verse—you'd be insane

or dead. You can't have the breadth of everyone's life lessons—just the panorama of your own. It's not that you keep making the same mistake . . . you are participating in versions of the same structures. Your impatience keeps them coming.

"What? You again?" Do you then stamp your feet or slam the door? You will learn the difference which patience makes. Rather than greeting those redundancies with dread—you welcome them as old friends and ask them to teach you what they can. You really must become more courteous (invite them in) and patient (learn from them—don't hurry to send them away). As it is now, you want to be all over the map. Everywhere at once. Accomplishing. Achieving. Perfecting. Inventing. Inspiring. In case you haven't noticed, you are tired. You simply need to stop working so hard. Walking so fast. Your impatience to taste everything keeps you from tasting anything.

So. Yes. You do learn. And you will learn by embracing paradox. In unlearning you learn. In slowing down you fly. In welcoming trouble you see those troubles less often. Allow the events of your life to not make sense. That is the only way they can ever make sense.

You ask if I am happy. So I will tell you. No, I am not happy. I see the world too clearly to be happy. But I am content. And I think that is a better thing.

Be kind to yourself. Stop waiting to grow up: you never will. You only grow and that's a more vital process than "growing up." I love you, Mary Anne.

Yes, the letter was from me to myself. I wrote "myself" at seventy-eight a letter and asked if I ever learn to stop making the same mistakes.

What advice would Gina at seventy-eight give you? What do you want to ask of her?

June 29, Gina writes:

I don't think you could have come closer to the target. The only hitch is that I'm constantly aware of my own impatience and (how's this for irony) even impetuousness. I don't think being aware of it changes its shape or how it plays out in my life, but at least I can point to it when I see it. I am impatient, even here where I have so much to potentially absorb and learn— wait, probably more here when I have so much . . . people intrigue and briefly attract my attention, but I tire of them quickly. That's a little disconcerting sometimes, but I'm getting used to it. And maybe that's one reason I always tell myself "In the next place I'll find . . ." whatever it is.

I'm sitting by the river now, waiting for a woman from Peru. I told her I would teach her English. She's not around. I could have gone to the Smithsonian. This is kind of nice though. Still water—quiet, appearing patient. I'm tempted to go rent a kayak and go rowing. I'd rather just jump in (too dirty). Elie Wiesel wrote something about closing your eyes and leaping. Did you know that? (Great minds . . .)

July 9, my mother's birthday, I write to Gina:

Is the "whatever it is" you'll find in the next place, intimacy? I wonder—and here's why. I've been contemplating this issue in regard to myself. I have a lifetime preference for periods of isolation. Prefer reading to movies. Conversation to games. Debate to conversation. I'd rather be doing something with a measurable or productive end. So many people bore me rather than interest me. I find quick judgment natural. Each of those things is an asset as well as a liability.

"Whatever it is" may have something to do with finding where you put that key that locked up so much of you . . . somewhere. I know. I locked up a lot of myself because the enormity of caring and feeling and seeing was simply too much to bear in light of so many losses. But from the vaporous threats of these days I am experiencing an odd flight. Almost a metamorphosis. The butterfly has been a significance to me since I moved south. Perhaps I finally cast away my cocoon and began to see the real color of my wings. Perhaps.

To my walking companion I said, "I like butterflies," as I extended my finger, gently, to the pausing monarch.

"Birds eat butterflies, don't they?" he asked.

I mused that this may be generally representative of the differences in our world views. I smiled at him and said, "I suppose if I were a bird, I could hardly restrain myself from eating a butterfly."

Beauty is often consumed.

Yes. To answer your earlier question, all rivers run to the sea and the blood that runs its course so red becomes clear in the enormity of the sea—the sea that cannot become full.

Gina moved back to her work in Uganda and we continued our correspondence via e-mail. But there is something about putting a pen to the scratch of paper that invites a different pace of writing and a differing way of communicating thought than the speed of e-mail.

Listen to your intuition: learn to trust it. Do not assume you should talk yourself out of listening to that inner voice. (How often have you said, in retrospect, "I had a funny feeling about that"?) *Listen!* In many instances you already know the answer to the question. Listen and benefit from criticism and praise. Do not defend. Do not deny. Consider well. Choose what you will keep and use. Choose what you will disregard with no further thought.

Learn to wait. Waiting is a skill. It is active, not passive. Waiting is exercising a unique control and also giving up control. This very paradox is what makes waiting effective. Waiting often produces more and better options. Waiting cools the fire of fury. Waiting introduces new ideas. It can eliminate the desire for something that may have appeared essential. Anthony Kesler has often asked me to consider, "What is the consequence of not acting?"

Consider the role preparation plays in protection. Measure the risks you are willing to take in order to achieve your sense of purpose. Identify different options in the process of defending yourself. Try walking away as a fine defense.

because i call it challenge rather than crisis; because i look at hardship as opportunity instead of obstacle; because at the end of a matter, i ask, "what will i learn from this to make me better?"; because i take a deep breath and do the difficult thing first; because my courage does not depend on the weather, the economic forecast, or the winds of whim; because i know the most significant elements in my day are laughter, learning, and applying my finest efforts to each endeavor; because of these things, each morning is a pleasure and every day passed is a success.

Twice

To embrace the fate my actions have created.
As a toreador his bull, ignoring the leaning crowds
And curses that gradually murder humility.
But rather hearing the ever patient whisper,
May I learn to bottle my humanity and live twice:
Once for the life I am and again for the heart I swallowed.

—*Conrad*

Conrad, a participant in my prison-based writing group, has captured for me in those last two sentences, something nearly ineffable. If we are fortunate, we each find our way to a redemption of the losses in our lives. The idea of living twice evokes a real sense of fullness partnered with self-reliance or personal accountability. The Leopoulos family could speak to this with certainty. The ability to discern an ever patient whisper in the midst of the press of a crowd is a key to not allowing your eyes to determine what you see. Some things can only be seen rightly with the heart.

Change is to our lives as water is to our bodies. Without it, we dry up, we die. It is the source. Change wakes us up in the morning. It is change that keeps us from sleeping through the best parts of our lives. Change is an unannounced window washer. We may not have known our windows were so filthy but once they are cleaned by the masterful hands of change we declare in awe, "Why, I've never seen this vista quite this way. And how did I manage not to notice that magnificent sycamore tree?"

Yes, change is an excellent window washer. Change frequently switches positions in our lives. Change has a resume by which anyone would be impressed:

> travel agent
> speech pathologist
> disease
> unexpected loss
> train wreck (difficult to explain: but everyone seems to
>   understand)
> annoying boss
> disrespectful teacher
> difficult dance partner.

Change often employs undesirable positions to accomplish his goals. He's been known to send ants to picnics. He's particularly fond of raining out pow-wows. He readily defends his actions, "Difficulty and I often work together. Although, I prefer to work alone. When I visit a person's day—they have the opportunity to be better, brighter, healthier. How I am welcomed all depends on the perspective of the person I am visiting."

When questioned about the rumored amounts of fear that his visits generate, change reluctantly acknowledges, "Yes, there does seem to be a fair amount of fear associated with my name. But it's a short-term condition. Once I am welcomed and someone truly experiences the remarkable results of my work, they learn to want me around. I get lots of return invitations, really! Ask anybody who's spent a first time with me. They'll tell you their lives were pretty predictable and joyless before they embraced me."

Change smiled, but then looked somewhat melancholy. "I told you I prefer to work alone. Really, I do. I would rather not ask Difficulty to come along with me on a job. It's a great day when someone sees me for who I really am and invites me along. I bring Difficulty into the work only as a last choice. I love going to job sites on my own. It's how I do my most effective work. But, when people can't pay attention to what I need to accomplish, I'll go ahead and bring Difficulty along just to get their attention."

If all things in my life are lessons, what am I learning? Things are not usually as they appear. No one is truly seen by another. Everyone views everything through their own life experiences, fears, longings, and expectations. Regularly regarded beliefs and closely held assumptions are barriers to discovery and innovation. Being so certain of all you know is a type of blindness. Uncertainty is a way to fuller seeing on a new journey. It's when you're absolutely certain you know all the turns that you are most likely to get lost.

Ask yourself, "Will this matter to me in a month, six months, a year?" Measure your immediate response appropriately. Consider any challenge in the context of the greater events of your life, or in the context of the types of challenges that others, less fortunate than you, deal with daily. Measure your response. Ask yourself what you can learn from this circumstance. Wait twenty-four hours to discover if what seems so significant right now matters as much to you at this same time tomorrow.

I play with words. I play in my thinking. I like telling stories about things . . . it is play for me to turn a word or an idea around in a way I've never seen before. I like asking words to do things they don't usually do. It's fun.

My father, whose favorite flower was the simple and truthful daisy, spoke of remembered priorities and the single regret of his life at his dying. He said, "I worked too damn hard. I would have played more if I had known how the memories would sit with me."

the isle of skye:
a pretending poem for molly
if i had been born
on the isle of skye
(which is a place in
scotland, by the by)

so . . .

if i had been born
on that isle of skye
i would skip. i would jump.
and then i would fly.

i would fly to the land.
i would fly to the sea.
i'd come visit you and
you'd come with me.

you'd come with me
to the isle of skye
(remember, it's in scotland . . .
i don't know why).

you would come with me
and far we would sail.
and we would play, you see,
with the birds and a whale.
we'd fly to the land.
we'd fly to the sea.
we'd go see our friends but
they could not be

as light as we
are up in the air . . .
they could not see.
they would not dare.

so . . .
you'd come back with me
to the isle of skye
(which is in scotland;
do you know why?).

and we play the wind.
and we laugh the moon.
and we whisper the rain.
and dance 'til it's june.

we fly to the night
and rise with the day.
we roll out the breakers.
we know how to play!

we know how to play
on this isle of skye
(which we know is in scotland,
we don't much care why).

we don't really care
about the what or the why
when we think of scotland
holding our dear isle of skye.

it simply does
(it's that plain)
that's how it is
(it's that true)
it doesn't keep me from flying.
it doesn't keep me from you.

so, let's pretend . . .

we were born
on the isle of skye
(which is a place in
scotland, by the by).

since we were born
in that isle of skye . . .
we will skip and we'll jump
and then we will fly.

we will fly
down the staircase.
we will fly
out the door.
we will fly
to our friend's house.
we will fly
ever more.

ever more we are
flying over
sea, over stone.
ever more i'll
fly with you
from the skye
to our home.

Just like clothing, play looks different on different people. The commonality of play is found in this: that one wholly, without reservation (ah, with abandon) gives oneself over to something one utterly loves doing. This is how what looks like play to one person is work to another. (I've often said that jumping out of a perfectly good airplane is too much work to be fun for me.)

Hauling my hips around in soil for seven hours, ripping out what I mostly hope to be weeds and digging holes and rooting things from small plastic planters into those holes is hard, physical labor. Terry Hershey finds it restful and meditative. Personal choice and clear preference is at the core of play.

The gardener I mentioned, Terry Hershey, is the author of *Soul Gardening, Sacred Necessities* and several other books. He is a highly effective trainer and speaker. I consider Terry an expert at what I'm going to call guerilla play. There you are, certain he's being cynical, or serious, or quite busy at respectable work and quite unexpectedly, he's at play. It can happen anywhere. At anytime. When you least anticipate it. In Terry's company, you find yourself laughing: at him, at something (or somebody) else, and, most often, at yourself. I caught a whiff of a poem of Raymond Carver's called "Malinger." Immediately I sent it to Terry. I knew that he, as an expert on guerilla play and a committed student of doing nothing, well, would appreciate it. You come to see, beyond choice and preference, sometimes play is practicing the art of doing nothing.

Play

Today is an ordinary Sunday. I'm sitting outside at my patio table. There are remnants of the *New York Times,* an empty coffee mug, and a blank notepad with a pen. My assignment is to write about play. I wrestle with the automatic knee jerk compulsion to want to say the right thing. Something important. But it gets caught up in the maelstrom of cultural expectations about performance and it makes my head hurt. So I get another cup of coffee.

Out on the lawn, my eight-year-old son, Zach, is sketching a Western Red Tanager. The Tanager (a male with a vibrant red and yellow jacket) spent the morning splashing in our pond. We don't see Tanagers much, so when they make an appearance, everything else on the to-do list gets demoted. My notepad is still blank. There is too much swirling in my head to organize my thoughts, so I take a break and wander down to one of my garden beds where a David Austin rose has bowed to the weight of blooms, all canes akimbo, doing its best imitation of the Scarecrow from the *Wizard of Oz*. It needs staking, and I notice a convention of bees delighting in the hardy geranium nearby, entertaining themselves with a musical mantra, some kind of a monastic a cappella chant. I take a hit of the rose, a concoction of cloves and some unnameable soap from my childhood, which all reminds me of last night's meal, Chicken Adobo in garlic and soy and white vinegar, with a 1996 Domaine Tempier Bandol Bordeaux made in heaven, or at least that part of France that is closest to heaven. So I walk back to the house to see if there's any wine remaining, pausing to watch one of our cats chase a butterfly, until he admits defeat and rolls for a spell in the gravel, basking in the afternoon sun. Back in my chair on the patio, I sip my Bordeaux, the perfumed *terroir* of spring earth and compost, and watch Zach and his friend run through the sprinkler on the lawn. They squeal. Literally. It seems they live by the philosophy that if the day doesn't have a game worth playing, it's a good time to make one up. I want to ask them what play means, but there's some cosmic rule about interrupting anyone who is actively enthralled.

I realize that I have conveniently forgotten to stake the rose.

If I were pressed, I would say that play is living without an agenda. But that almost sounds like some kind of a dictum. And I swear by the philosophy that any time we reduce life to a one-sentence dictum, it's time to de-tox. For me it is garden ambling, sometimes with a nine iron in my hand, to practice my golf swing and whack a couple of stray practice golf balls into the woods. I have a friend who kayaks in the eddies and canals that connect all the lakes in central Florida, another who sits on his boat around midnight out in the inter-coastal waters in total darkness and listens to music under the stars, another who hikes in the woods where the trees are the size of cathedrals and the earth smells of history and rain, and still another who goes fishing without really caring whether he catches anything. Apparently, it's just the fishing that seems to matter.

I read a great story about a research project with children. The children were put into a room with new toys. Psychologists and social scientists watched them from another room. The study was to determine which toys they enjoyed most. After twenty minutes or so of playing with all the new toys, the children spent the remainder of their time enthusiastically playing with . . . the boxes that the toys came in.

It makes me laugh out loud just to picture it. Children are wired to be fully alive. To see. Wired to derive joy from that which is simple. It is a byproduct of engagement. There is no need for stuff to entertain, or occupy, or preoccupy, or distract. To put it another way, someone once said that miracles are simply being in the right place at the right time. And kids see miracles in simple boxes. Somewhere along the way to adulthood, something gums up the system.

And that something is happening to people younger and younger. I read a recent statement by a nine-year-old boy who said he wanted to "be inside because that's where all the electrical outlets are." There's no advantage to taking a moral high road here, but something tells me that "indoor play" is an oxymoron.

Here's the straight scoop: Play, if it is anything, is a sensual fiesta. It means being alive in this world—to exude playfulness squarely in the sights, sounds, smells, and tastes of this day.

Did you see the movie *Ray* (the story of Ray Charles)? There is a great scene where Ray Charles is having lunch with Della Bea, the women who will become his wife. She wonders about his blindness.

Ray says, "I hear like you see. Like that hummingbird outside the window, for instance."

Della is amazed, "I can't hear her."

"You have to listen," says Ray.

Della closes her eyes, hears the hummingbird, and says, "Yes."

Scott Russell Sanders observed that "for the enlightened few, the world is always lit." Which is another way of saying that the requirement for enlightenment is pretty straight forward: let yourself live like a kid. So it boils down to this: simple pleasures. What Rudolph Otto referred to as "Mysterium Tremendum." Translated, it means "the bare mystery of simply being." Or, in the words of C. S. Lewis, talking about joy, "I was overwhelmed by spine-tingling elation."

Do you know G. K. Chesterton's story of the teenage boy granted a wish by a genie: to be huge or tiny? We are all swayed by the appeal of being big, strong, and powerful. So the boy chose huge. The outcome was predictable: in a few hours the boy was bored. Because of his size, he walked around the world in only a few steps. Scaled the largest mountains. Like any child thirty minutes after the presents are opened, "Is that all there is?"

You see, Chesterton goes on to say, only "tiny people" can celebrate and enjoy life. Tiny people have nothing to prove, no score to settle, no one to impress. They approach each day, not from power or the need to dominate or defeat, but from respect. They have the freedom to receive. To live playful. Tiny people see God incognito in the everyday stuff of life. To squeal, under the spell of simple pleasures:

Watching my son dance to the Beatles
Hunting the woods for fresh flowers for the dining room table
Going barefoot in the summer
Belly laughter
Listening to the dawn
Running through the sprinkler
Planting a flower
Asking a stupid question
Hug from a child
Ring-side seats at a butterfly cabaret
Eating a big scoop of Ben and Jerry's ice cream
The rich smell of the earth after a spring rain
Tears during a good movie
The lick of a golden retriever

Filtered sunlight through the morning bedroom window
Memories of childhood: bacon frying, lilacs in May, Sunday
pot-roast, and the aroma from my grandfather's pipe.

In such a moment, there is that stab of well-being straight to
the marrow of our bones, and we know it, and sense it, but
find ourselves unable to describe it, or write about it, or teach
it for that matter, which is all well and good, because we keep
it free from the panel of judges that call the shots on whether
life is worth living.

Of this much I am certain: Like everything else, our culture
has turned play into some sort of an achievement, a contest,
a beauty pageant. And in the end, it kind of defeats the point.

So we treat play as if it is a problem to be solved, and
we counter with a book on play for dummies redolent with
activity-appropriate checklists. As if play is something to be
accomplished. We add play to our jitterbug of activities, feeling duly accomplished with our new-found ability to multi-
task. Sure, we want to play, but feel compelled to buy the right
clothes before we get started. I read that in this culture we
worship our work, play at our worship, and work at our play.
That rings true. I do know that we put an accomplishment tag
on just about everything we do. Hence our tendency to make
play and wasted time synonymous. Living oblivious to the
Jewish heritage of Sabbath, which reminds us there is one day
a week, set aside, to literally, waste time with God.

Play as a synonym for romping in and reveling in the day's
simple pleasures is a tough sell in a "never-enough world" with
this onslaught of choices. That's what happens with speed,
this crush of information with our "can't miss" technology

guaranteed to give us more time. In the end we live out of breath and out of time.

And we see less,
taste less,
listen less,
smell less,
touch less,
and savor our own fullness less.

Which begs the question: How do we re-train our own eye (or mind) to appreciate simple pleasures? To play? To live playful? Is there a spiritual practice that we can incorporate into our lives that opens our eyes to the abundant simple pleasures that surround us?

Let's begin with this: Can you tell me a simple pleasure that happened, that you enjoyed, in the past hour? The past day?

And while we're on the subject, it wouldn't hurt to change the way we talk to one another. We ask, of each other, daily, "What do you do?" Or, "What did you do?" Why not ask, "What surprised you today?" "What made you smile?" "What sprinklers did you run through today?"

We live in a world with two spaces. One for accomplishment, checklists, busyness, and doing. The other is about being. And play. It is the space where music, laughter, friendship, enchantment, and wonder are birthed and nourished. Or, in the words of Flora Colao, "we need to play so that we can rediscover the magical around us."

So it's not really about play. It's about being awake.

Listen to Henry David Thoreau's two cents. "Nothing can be more useful to a man (or woman) than a determination not to be hurried."

Sure, I want to play, I want to live this moment mindful of the sacred, but this is not the time or the day for it. As if there is a special day for it. I'll play if I can program it into my Blackberry. And in our western mind-set, play (or living in the present) becomes a staged event. As if this is something we must orchestrate. Or arrange. And we sit stewing in the juices of our self-consciousness. Am I playing yet? What am I doing right or wrong? All the while, missing the point, which is to be . . . open.

Available.

Curious.

Willing to be surprised by joy.

It is late afternoon. The sun is still narcotic warm.

Hummingbirds cajole each other at the feeder. My son wants me to pitch wiffle, ball and I had some great insight about play I wanted to capture before it is unretrievable in the clutter of my mid-life mind. It was going to be really important. But I can't recall it.

I pitch to my son. He hits the ball. He cheers as he runs to first base. Whatever my new-found insight, it can wait for another day.

Willfully choose play. Hang out with some children if you need reminding. Allow your play to contribute to your sense of being as well as your labor does. Remember play need not be complex or long. Take advantage of playful moments. Again, observe children if you need help with this.

days are winged and my promise flies before me.
you are invited to stand up tall into the whole possibility of
    yourself and breathe out your wonder upon the world.

there are many ways to see a mountain.
there are many ways to embrace folly and become wise.
there are many ways to know the power of your own fire.
there are many ways to celebrate winter and walk into spring.
there are many ways to wrap yourself in red and fly.
many ways.
there are many ways to pen a lyric, and raise your voice
    and sing.
there are many ways to be a mountain.

The lamp has a high-pitched buzz as if it is working strenuously to bring me this half light. My head rests in my palm
and my eyes fall to the words I have painted on the wall:
*It is not the critic who counts, not the man who points out
how the strong man stumbled or where the doer of deeds could
have done them better.*

*The credit belongs to the man who is actually in the arena;
whose face is marred by dust and sweat and blood; who strives
valiantly; who errs and comes up short again and again; who
knows the great enthusiasms, the great devotions, and spends
himself in a worthy cause.*

*Who at best knows, in the end, the triumph of high
achievements; and who at the worst, if he fails, at least fails
while daring greatly so that his place shall never be with those
cold and timid souls who know neither victory nor defeat.*
                                        —*Theodore Roosevelt*

I need to celebrate that I am fresher, stronger, renewed, reinvented, have chosen not to be gripped by my history, the hurt, the disloyalty, the lack of place—this bitterness would only lead to illness, to unproductive days. Rather than say this is what I do not want, let me instead assert what I do want: I want to embrace the holy opportunity of each moment. I have to create new structures with knowledge and foundation and focus.

I can be the woman I most admire. All those qualities are within my grasp. I can grow in strength and stature. I can celebrate my quiet spirituality. I can walk through fires and stand unharmed. Because no one can damage my spirit without my permission.

Telling the truth has all kinds of risks associated with it but not telling the truth is riskier. Remind yourself to function from a place of purpose and intention. Live a life that inspires yourself and others. If there is good able to come from your hand, give it. Good for yourself and good for others. Speak the truth and celebrate it. Even though it may be a hard truth. Be content in your focus, stand tall and love your life as it is. Remember to walk just in this moment. With one breath following another. And in the walk, strengthen your sense of purpose and then lean into your life. Whisper to yourself: "Gentle soul, understand the longing of your life has already been answered. Each day is a gift to be unwrapped. It falls to your grace, your maturity, to understand the nature of the gift once it is opened."

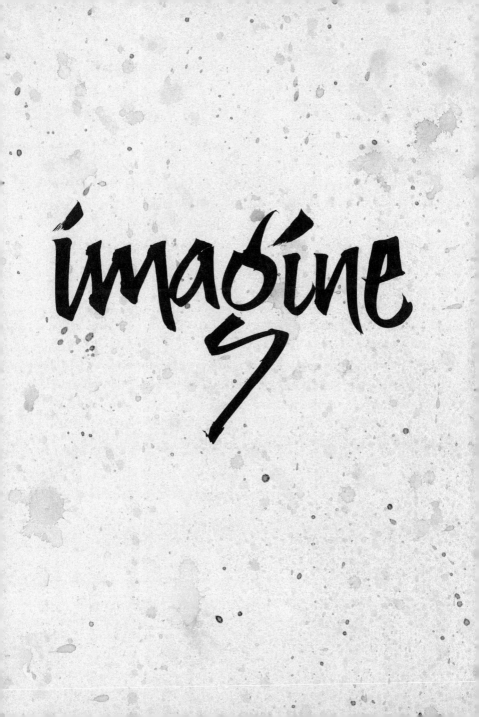

Thank you, Emily, for these winged words which I often whisper to myself.

Hope is the thing with feathers that perches in the soul and sings the tune without the words and never stops at all.
—*Emily Dickinson*

And sometimes poetry can make a whole, sound, and healthy person cry because the words, crafted well, have a ring of hope and truth to them, which transcends intellect and reaches beyond simple emotion. And when poetry does that it sings the tune without the words.

Just the other day I outlined a seemingly unlikely scenario to my friend Suze, who giggled and assessed, "That's some fantasy." I quickly explained, "This isn't a fantasy . . . this is simply reality in training."

Noah Singer is an amazing young man headed for—well—the stars. I could have called him stellar and that would have summed it up. Noah works, lives, and breathes in the world of competitive biking. But you can ask the folks in his world: he finds time to love all of them. He has a very practical experience to share about what it is to imagine. Noah writes:

"If your opponent is bigger, faster, and stronger; train longer, harder, and smarter."
—*H. Jackson Brown, Jr.*

Throughout my short career there have been the ups and downs associated with every victory and defeat. When I was getting into the sport of competitive cycling in 2000 my dad gave me a book by H. Jackson Brown, Jr., titled *A Hero in*

Every Heart. Since then that little book has been to almost every race, both physically and mentally. I once heard that training is 90 percent physical and 10 percent mental, while racing is 90 percent mental and 10 percent physical. At the elite level it seems to me that almost all of the athletes are on the same page physically. Yes, some are at the top of the page and some are at the bottom, but they are all there. What sets apart the continuous winners from the back of the pack is the mental game played on and off the field.

When I race I play a mental game which lasts from the night before to the night after the event. When I go to bed on race eve I think about what I will be doing tomorrow and how much pain I will be putting myself through. I smile. When I get to the start line I act like I am showing up for a normal Saturday morning training ride and there is no reason to be nervous. Then I think of every single training ride, every mile, every climb, and every sprint I did to prepare for this very moment. I reassure myself I am completely prepared and there is nothing to worry about.

And, there isn't.

I start not only every race like this, but every day of my life—with a lot of confidence followed by a nice cup of coffee. Whether the day before was good or bad, I start anew and focus on what is to come. You must look forward, yes, lean forward, into your life.

Gina had transferred from service in Uganda to a humanitarian-aide position in Darfur, Sudan. Daily I rehearsed my confidence in her choices and believed the finest net of safety to be wrapped about her. Often I would send reports of Gina's activities to my friend Tina and take comfort that she and her band of prayer warriors would hold their light on Gina's path. I wanted everyone to remind all the angels they knew to cast a caring eye toward Gina on the other side of the world. The other side of the world living in conditions so removed from my own I am tempted to call them "other" worldly. But they are the means of ordinary life experiences for the people there, displaced by war and daily placed in harms way meeting the demands of lack, hunger, war, and misplaced promises.

As she prepared to return to America for an extended visit I welcomed her with these words:

Like a scarf carefully chosen and wrapped around my shoulders, I have worn thought of you and care for you every day. As you return to the dichotomous opulence and oppression of America, I wear my thought of you no less. Perhaps even greater is the need for your friends to hold you high upon their shoulders.

You return having your hearing pulled and pummeled, having your vision challenged in both the literal and metaphorical view, having your ethics as an America child tried in the court of international abuse and assumption. Atrocities pass for sound bites in the worlds where you have muddied yourself—if such even makes it to the news desk. Thirty-seven reporters flank a self-indulgent pop star's visit to the bathroom or hair color change; rape, illness of extraordinary magnitude, and disease go unchecked. Prejudice-wielding weapons such as these and more to fill pages populate a country where barely a single reporter walks. The contrast in priority is staggering and its core goes so much deeper than the color of the skin being covered. It does, however, in spite of what we want to admit, begin with the color of the skin.

As you return to this place, the verdant geography, the exquisite dinner table, the sterile bathrooms, there is a scarf I suggest you wear. The scarf of compassion and temperance. You have seen a people without legs. Know now you are in the company of a people who take their walking for granted. Your compassion must help you channel your anger. The contrast is great. But it is, of course, greater for you for what you have seen and touched and lived among.

In this reentry, cry your tears with your trusted hearts and let the movement of your pen heal your wounds as it measures itself across the page.

You bring change. You are a wind of change; know where you walk. Be a wise zephyr rather than a turbulence of grand disturbance. Direct the storm of what you have seen into ways that manifest change. And that leads to Gandhi's most difficult offering: "Be the change you wish to see in the world."

Enjoy the food. The softness of your bed. The absence of insects crawling about you. These components will be absent from you repeatedly. That they are present to you now is a blessing. A holiday to your knowing of how simply most of the world lives. In this day you may live simply, too, without condemning the excesses, which will greet you on every road.

I remember weeping in the grocery store the day after a return from a long sojourn in Italy. The food is shadow food—I saw, really, for the first time. It is shallow. It has no soil holding to it. It has no memory of the real taste. The real taste of a potato has been engineered from its recollection long ago. And from the palettes who ingest it and mindlessly call it a potato.

In some of the same way, Americans are living shadow lives. Stuffing in the cracks of their days shreds of acquisition and televised blather to keep the light from seeping in.

Imagine that you are a light.

You will shine—sometimes fired by anger and judgment and other times with compassion and a greater grasp of what, ultimately, cannot be understood or explained. Living with such paradox increasingly becomes one of the unique challenges of your life.

Leaning forward—knowing where you are going and how to get there even though you've never been there before; catching an unexpected fast-moving object with your left hand even though you're right handed, even though you weren't really looking; calling a friend with just your heart not a phone; doing a first-time thing in front of others without fear; saying YES! before you know the whole question just because you know who's asking the question; knowing an irrevocable certainty about the high regard for your circle.

The art of living well is tied so closely to living artfully. And as I step from one day to the next I offer myself my own letter of welcome led with these ideas:

You are empirical evidence of the presence of God.

You are a demonstration of the manifestation of the divine.

Your relationship to spirit is beyond structure.

Let go of the ties that would define and restrict your heart and you will begin your divine discovery. You will soar.

inspiration dawns at unlikely times and dreams come true far away from clocks and calendars.

dream big. and if you can't manage BIG just dream little . . . because dreams have a way of growing.

Ask yourself, "What if I did one thing differently today." (What can I do differently today?) And then be certain to ask yourself, "How is it I would like to remember this day?" for certainly, this day is your own legacy.

What if I just believed a little lean of my wing feathers could change the direction of my flight?

What if I just acted like everything was easy?

What if I just made a point of laughing right out loud?

What if I was certain I knew what I needed?

Perhaps it is this day my dreams awaken me by name and I answer, yes.

Perhaps it is this day I have the courage to trade my "is" for the "if."

Perhaps it is this very day I resolve to pass on the answers and go straight for the most excellent and meaningful questions.

Perhaps . . .

it is this day I will lean forward into my life.

afterword
a commonplace book for an uncommon life

Throughout this book I have referenced the value writing has had in my own life. There are so many books available on the subject of personal journal writing—writing your way to a deeper knowing of your self, your purpose.

I've met so many people whose hands just freeze up when they instruct themselves to write in their journal. Here, I have another suggestion. A commonplace book.

A commonplace book has been a practice in learned societies for hundreds of years. It perhaps was at its zenith in the Renaissance but continued as a vital tool of personal learning and moral development for centuries after.

The commonplace book became, essentially, a personal catalog of significant lessons, philosophy, concepts, and ways of knowing. In it, hand-transcribed passages from speeches, readings, poetry, and debates would be entered and reflected upon. It came about in days when writing materials were precious, books were even more precious, and learning was often a personal responsibility. It was a tool endorsed by some key philosophers.

In American history we have such recognizable figures as George Washington, Thomas Jefferson, and Ralph Waldo Emerson who maintained this practice, and we learn much of their epistemology by the contents of their commonplace books. In revolutionary America, learning was considered a lifelong pursuit. John Adams, for example, rarely simply read a book. He read and reflected. He allowed the words of another to become incorporated into his own knowledge base. It would be from that reflection that summary would be entered into a commonplace book.

Ralph Waldo Emerson kept a lifelong list of all the books he read. General Wesley Clark was moved to enlist in military service by a speech of John F. Kennedy. I know where I was when I first heard the lyrics to "I hope you dance" coming over the radio. I had to pull over to the side of the road and listen hard. Those words moved me deeply and infused me with a peculiar courage to face an imminent challenge. "There is a certain fire that no man can put out," are words that have reverberated throughout my life from when the assassination of Dr. Martin Luther King, Jr. brushed against the edges of my childhood. What phrases have become part of the fibers of your life?

What could you learn about yourself today if you had maintained a list of the books you had read since childhood and the main lessons that each of those books contained, the lyrics of music or poetry that moved you or caused you to change a specific way of knowing, speeches that moved you, current events that changed your view of the world, passages from a book that gave lightening insight into the reason behind your choices? What might keep you now from beginning such a record of your leaning and learning journey?

This book, which you hold in your hand, is essentially a version of my commonplace book. It contains words inspired by the thoughts and actions of others, lessons drawn after study, and notes to myself following significant life experiences that I might draw upon the memory of such a learning. (The writings have been featured on posters from my company, taken from many years of journal writing and various writing exercises and unpublished essays, as well as being created new written just for you.)

I have long held that any experience, regardless of its outcome, can be counted a success if I have learned something from it. From what many consider failures in my life I draw great strength and celebrate the ability to emerge from difficulty a little smarter and better equipped to cross the various busy intersections of my journey. The conclusions I draw from the successes of my life provide the framework for repeating those successes in the context of other experiences. Life is my schoolroom. The process of creating and maintaining a commonplace book becomes essentially like writing my own personal textbook.

As you begin your own commonplace practice, perhaps you will allow me to inspire you a little and provide a beginning place from which you can construct the mast of your own commonplace ship and fill your sails with the winds of reflection, courage, and the willingness to lean forward and learn forward into your life.

gratitudes (acknowledgments)

When I was little I got the best view of parades from atop the shoulders of my father. And I've had some of the finest views of my life hoisted to the shoulders of my friends. If you do not find your name here, just look at me; I wear your name every day.

Conari Press (Jan Johnson), my publisher; and Brenda Knight, my editor. You are my dream come true. Thank you for knocking on my door and telling me you want to see the books in me. All of the fine community of Conari have made me so happy that my writing is in their hands. (Such a talented community.)

The dear souls who have made my writing and art part of your homes and offices and school rooms and relationships over the last decades. You have been with me in my writing room and motivated me to move my pen.

Tina, Taylina, Anthony, and Tony, because much of what I write about family I have learned by watching yours. Tony, your words are peppered throughout this book and have seasoned my own leaning.

Kathy for choosing sisterliness and friendship, and John for that pink toy you gave me when I was eleven. And for loving on my dogs while I'm being bookish.

Amanda, for finishing my sentences correctly, Rachael and Susan and Jim and Dan for knowing my sentences before I say them.

Bramuccis in general and Gina specifically, each of you is served up neat and intoxicate me laughingly.

My super hero girls, Scrunchy Pants Kim and Blue Heron Suze, reality in training is so easy when it's with you two. And Jonathan and Suze—for the magic carpet you've given my words.

Doug, Ben, Gen, Craig, Connie, and Von for your friendship; it is a grace. Len, for your questions.

Peter Beren for using my journals and wanting my writing to have a voice.

Fay Gentle for giving so many writing hearts the key to their own room. My writing group: Terry Zion, Conrad, Thomas Curtis, Paul Daniel Tice, Daniel Ryel, Abu Sayid Abdurrashid Haytham Abdul Wadid, J.E. Wantz. Your unfettered talents, shared generously, have made me a better writer, and you all have helped me be a better person.

Lewis Lapham for telling such hard truth so well. And Al Gore, president Bill Clinton, Senator Hillary Rodham Clinton, Howard Zinn, Paul and Linda Leopoulos, Mary Oliver, Tom Cruise, Ben Linder, Shel Silverstein, and the finest of folks at NPR for the leadership of your lives.

Paul and Linda Leopoulos, Gina Bramucci, Rachael Bourdet, Jane Kirkpatrick, Michael R. Wigal, Terry D. Hershey, Noah Singer, Richard Kesler, Terry Zion, Conrad, Karah G. Fisher, and Lorrena Thompson for crafting such fine words and adding your voices to this book.

Meg, Amy, Chuck, and Joyce (for always believing); Louise, Bob and Cynthia, Curtis and Susan, Matie G. (for candles and quotes); Roxanne, Robbie, Janie, Shar, Paula, Lynn, Paul (for Sunday morning writing), Tracee (for yoga); Millie. Joyce, Gabriel, Kim, Cindy, Earl and Ruth (for the prayers); Lori, you are the exclamation points on the sentences of my days.

to our readers

Conari Press, an imprint of Red Wheel/Weiser, publishes books on topics ranging from spirituality, personal growth, and relationships to women's issues, parenting, and social issues. Our mission is to publish quality books that will make a difference in people's lives—how we feel about ourselves and how we relate to one another. We value integrity, compassion, and receptivity, both in the books we publish and in the way we do business.

Our readers are our most important resource, and we value your input, suggestions, and ideas about what you would like to see published. Please feel free to contact us, to request our latest book catalog, or to be added to our mailing list.

Conari Press
An imprint of Red Wheel/Weiser, LLC
500 Third Street, Suite 230
San Francisco, CA 94107
www.redwheelweiser.com